THE HANDWEAVER'S PATTERN BOOK

Over 120 Designs for Upholstery, Curtains, Place Mats, etc.

IONA PLATH

Photographs by the Author

DOVER PUBLICATIONS, INC.
NEW YORK

Published in Canada by General Publishing Company, Ltd., 30 Lesmill Road, Don Mills, Toronto, Ontario.
Published in the United Kingdom by Constable and Company, Ltd., 10 Orange Street, London WC2H 7EG.

This Dover edition, first published in 1981, is an unabridged republication of *The Craft of Handweaving,* published by Charles Scribner's Sons, New York, in 1972. *The Craft of Handweaving* was published first in slightly different form by Charles Scribner's Sons, New York, in 1964 under the title *Handweaving.* In the present edition, the Handweaving Yarn Supply Sources and Loom Supply Sources have been updated, and a list of periodicals has been added.

International Standard Book Number: 0-486-24166-1
Library of Congress Catalog Card Number: 81-66301

Manufactured in the United States of America
Dover Publications, Inc.
180 Varick Street
New York, N.Y. 10014

CONTENTS

KEY TO PATTERNS ON COVER

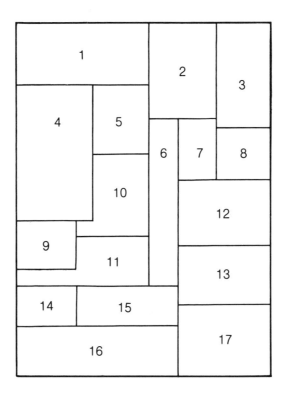

INTRODUCTION

This book presents handweaving as a useful craft and a fascinating hobby. It is a pattern book with intent to help homeweavers produce fabrics for their homes and families. It is written for the person who would like to weave, but hasn't the time or opportunity to study and devote hours to experimenting with designs and yarns before deciding on a pattern and materials.

Designing fabrics takes experience and a great deal of time. This is the field of the experienced or professional weaver. The homeweaver is not a professional, and for the most part, never intends to be. With a pattern and instructions anyone with little or no training can produce pleasing fabrics of sound construction. Learning to weave from patterns is an excellent way of gaining the knowledge necessary to go on to creating your own designs.

The designs chosen for the book are based on the type of patterns pupils have expressed a desire to weave, and from the most frequently ordered custom woven fabrics.

Since this is not a text book on the technique of weaving, many of the old colonial and other traditional patterns have been omitted. Emphasis is on contemporary design and texture, with many two and four harness threadings in plain and twill weaves, the design growing out of the character of the yarn. Many of the more intricate weaves are based on traditional patterns interpreted in new types and colors of yarns. Of these, the pillow design on page 55 was taken from an old Danish toweling weave; inspiration for the curtain on page 36 was a Swedish bedspread, and so on.

The first chapter explains how to weave from the patterns. Yarn requirements are given for finished items and requirements per yard are given for yardage weaving. Actual size photographs of unusual novelty yarns are shown along with photographs of all the patterns. Listed are standard size yarns, their yardages and yarn supply sources. Catalogues can be ordered from the list of loom manufacturers.

Making the warp, warping the loom, threading, tie-up, treadling and weaving are all explained in detail along with drawings to illustrate the process of dressing the loom. Treadling is given for floor looms with a key for table looms.

The basic principle of weaving is

simply the weaving of a thread called "weft" through tightly stretched threads called "the warp," as in darning. This weave is called tabby or plain weave, and there are over twenty designs in the book based on this simple weave. Although only a two harness loom is required for plain weave, it can be woven on a four harness loom, or a loom with any number of harnesses.

To weave patterns, the weft passes over or under different sets of warp threads, the number determined by the chosen pattern. To accommodate the different combinations of warp threads, a loom with four or more harnesses is required. Except for the designs in plain weave, most of the patterns in the book are for four harness looms. A few five, six and eight harness patterns are included for multiple harness weaving.

For handloom weaving, a loom is necessary to hold the warp threads firmly in place to receive the weft. The warp is threaded through eyes in long needle-like heddles which are arranged in frames called "harnesses." Different harnesses are raised according to plan, to form an opening between warp threads called "the shed," through which a shuttle with the weft yarn is passed. The harnesses are raised by hand levers on table looms, and by foot pedals on floor looms. The foot pedals can be tied to the harnesses so as to raise more than one at a time for pattern weaving. The same patterns can be woven on table looms by depressing more than one lever at a time.

The hobby weaver may find a table loom more convenient because it takes up less space. Considerable weaving can be accomplished in even a few spare moments although the hand-operated levers slow progress somewhat.

Floor looms with harnesses manipulated by foot pedals leave the hands free for weaving.

Since weaving width is determined by the width of the loom, a floor loom is necessary for those wishing to weave wide yardages. Floor looms come in many widths, a 36" to 45" width being the most practical.

It does not necessarily follow that the smaller the loom, the easier to operate. It is not at all essential that the beginner start with a small loom and work up to a larger one. The beginner can learn to weave on a four harness, six pedal floor loom as easily as on a smaller one, as the principle is the same for all looms.

The considerations involved in the purchase of a loom are those of any other piece of equipment—space, price, and purpose.

Handweaving is a useful craft when you consider that tweeds, draperies, curtains, rugs, upholsteries, accessories and other small items can all be woven on a handloom. Your handwoven fabrics will be distinguished from power-loomed products by an individual character and the stamp of your own personality.

All weavers get inspiration for other weaves as they work, and that is the time to plan for the next project. Always keep your loom warped. When a web has been finished and cut from the loom, be ready to warp for the next, even though you may not plan to begin weaving at once. You will be surprised how many times you will sit down to weave.

A loom folded and put away in a closet is not going to be used very often. Actually a loom is an attractive object and certainly a conversation piece. A shelf of bright colored yarns is decorative as well as inspiring. The family or hobby room in today's house is an ideal place for a loom permanently set up for weaving. At any rate, the place for the loom should be in or near the room where we spend the greater part of our time.

TO WEAVE FROM THE PATTERNS

The Rising Shed Loom The first thing you will want to know about this or any weaving pattern book is what type of loom the book is written for. This book is written for a jack-type rising shed loom. Most floor looms today are of this type, and all table looms with hand levers are rising shed looms.

If the loom is a counter-balance type with a sinking shed, the weaver will tie the blank spaces instead of the crosses in the tie-up. The loom then will weave the same patterns. The only difficulty will arise when weaving non-balanced patterns such as 3/1 twill. An attachment known as a shed regulator may be obtained which will give a higher open shed making possible non-balanced weaving.

The simplest way to find out which type of loom you have is to tie one heddle frame to one pedal. Tread this pedal. If the frame goes up independently, the loom has a rising shed.

For table looms, the tie-up is not necessary. Depressing the levers, one at a time, will show that each frame rises independently, making it a rising shed loom.

Photos The black and white photos are actual size so that picks per inch may be counted, and yarn substitutions made. All pictures show warp running vertically, and weft horizontally, as it would be seen on the loom. To note the weft order, start at the bottom of the picture and read up, the same as it would be woven.

2 Harness Looms The number of harnesses and pedals required are given for each pattern. Many of the 4 harness weaves may be done on a 2 harness loom such as those on pages 20, 24, 27, 31, 32, 39, 40, 41, 43, 45, 62, 64, 65, 71, 73, 78, 85, 96, 100, 110, 123. The threading is the same for frames 1 and 2. Change the threading of frames 3 and 4 back to 1 and 2. Tread 1, 2. The result will be the same.

(7)

Warp Yarn Yardages per pound are given for warp yarns. To substitute another type of yarn, select one that has approximately the same number of yards per pound. Two small size yarns may be substituted for a larger size yarn if they total the same yardage per pound as the larger size. The two are heddled and dented together as one yarn. Example: use two ends of 16/2 cotton @ 6720 yards per lb., heddled together in place of one end of 8/2 @ 3360 yards per lb., single in a heddle. The warp will have twice as many ends as called for in the pattern. The effect will be only slightly different, producing a fabric that is a bit flatter. This may or may not be the effect wanted, and only a sample will show what the substitution will produce.

Warp Length To determine the length of the warp, total the finished yardage wanted, plus take-up and loom allowance. To this add any extra amount needed for hems, fringe, samples, etc.

Take-up varies, but an added 5" per yard is usually enough. If there is doubt, the first of the weaving is measured on the loom under tension. Release the tension, and measure again. The difference is the take-up which must be allowed for.

Add one yard for loom allowance. This allowance is for the end of the warp behind the heddles which cannot be rolled forward and woven, and for the tie-in at the start of weaving. If several cut-offs and re-tyings are to be made, this too must be added to the warp's length. Example. Six yards of weaving wanted, plus 30", plus one yard for the loom, equals 7 yards, 30 inches. An eight yard warp is called for.

Warp Width The total warp ends are given for each pattern for the width of the warp in the reed. If a width other than the one given is wanted, a different number of warp ends will be required. To determine the number of warp ends needed for a wanted width: multiply the width by the ends per inch. Example: 20" width @ 15 ends per inch, 20 × 15 equals 300 warp ends needed. Selvage ends, if any, are added to this figure, and in the case of a balanced pattern design, extra ends required for balance are also added.

There will be a difference in the width of the fabric off the loom, and the width of the warp in the reed. This is known as take-in, or draw-in which occurs during weaving, and must be calculated when deciding the width of the warp. For most home furnishing fabrics a 2" allowance is ample. Example: the 20" warp width above will weave into a fabric approximately 18" wide.

Considerably more take-in will occur in woolen warps, which is explained further under Fashion Fabrics.

To Calculate Warp Yarn Required After the warp ends and length have been established, the number of yards of yarn needed to make the warp are determined by multiplying the two figures. Example: a 3 yard warp wanted @ 300 ends; 3 × 300 equals 900 yards needed. Always order more yarn than the figure indicates. An extra 5% will often be needed. It is safer to order more than may be needed, for obvious reasons. In this case the amount would total 945 yards. Yarns come in 2, 4 or 8 ounce tubes, or one pound cones, and some yarns come in skeins. The yardage of weaving yarns per pound is stated on sample cards supplied by dealers. The amount to order is calculated from this yardage figure.

Warping Order Only in warp striped patterns is color order given as none is needed for a solid color warp.

The number in front of the color is the number of ends to warp of that particular color. If there is a number behind the color it refers to the number of times the sequence should be warped.

Example: 1 yellow wool } ×12
                1 yellow silk }

This would read, 24 alternating ends of silk and wool. Should there be a number before the group such as:

$$\times 4 \left\{ \begin{array}{l} \text{1 yellow wool} \\ \text{1 yellow silk} \\ \text{1 yellow wool} \end{array} \right\} \times 12$$

24 alternate ends of wool and silk plus one end wool times 4 or 100 ends are indicated.

After the striped warp is made, care must be taken that the warp is beamed with the first end to the right as you face the loom. Otherwise the stripe will be in reverse. This may or may not detract from the general effect of the fabric, but it will have a different character than planned.

Weft Yarns Most certainly many substitutions will be made in weft yarns, especially in the decorative fabrics and pillows.

Lacking yarns large enough, the size may be built up by combining several smaller size yarns to give the required girth. A study of the actual size photographs will give some indication of the size yarns used. Unusual weft yarns are shown on pages 124 – 126. These will be of further help in the selection of yarns.

Many novelty yarns may or may not be available at the time of weaving, but again, substitutions can easily be made by comparing yarns on hand with those photographed.

To Calculate Weft Yarn Required To determine the amount of weft yarn needed, multiply the width in inches by the number of weft threads per one inch. This figure times 36 is the amount needed for one yard. This figure times the number of yards to be woven plus 5% for safety gives the amount of yarn needed. Example: 20" width in reed times 15 weft shots per one inch equals 300" or 8 yards 12 inches of weft yarn are needed for each inch. Multiplied by 36" gives 300 yards, which is the amount needed for one yard. This figure times the number of yards to be woven plus 5% equals the total number of weft yards required. A check with yards per pound of yarn will show how many pounds are needed.

In the case of a striped weft pattern, the plan is the same after noting the number of times each different yarn is used per inch.

Spooled Warps A person learning to weave may like to start with a table loom that comes equipped with a steel hexagon warp beam which will hold spools of prepared warp.

These 2" spools have warp ends of equal length. The spools are threaded onto the steel beam, the ends brought up and over the back beam, and threading may start.

This is an easy way to begin weaving, and if the size and colors of the yarns are those wanted for a particular pattern, the result will be the same as if a warp had been especially made.

The spools come in several colors of 20/2 cotton. There are 60 ends on the spool, each 20 yards long. At 30 ends per inch, each spool would equal 2" of warp. The width of the warp will determine the number of spools to use. Spools also come with 30 ends of 8/4 natural carpet warp, each end 10 yards long. The whole length need not be woven. Use as many yards as needed, cut off, and use the warp for a later project. Spools may be removed or left on the beam.

For warp to be made of other size yarns, and for mixed yarn warps, the traditional warp must be made.

There are many ways of going about this, but the following is a simple way, and will result in good warping.

Remove the beater and reed from the loom if possible.

Warping To make the warp, an extra piece of equipment is needed, such as a warping mill for long warps, or a warping frame (Fig. 1) for warps of ten yards or less. The principle is the same for both. Homeweavers will find the warping frame easier to use, less expensive, and more convenient, as it does not take up floor space. It may be used hung on the wall, or clamped to a table top. Most frames have a distance of one yard between pegs, the total giving a warp ten yards long. Pegs are skipped to make shorter warps.

To begin: tie the end of the warp to Peg X, carry to and under Peg Y, then in like manner, under Peg Z, and continue to Peg A. Now you will make the cross that will keep the warp in order for threading. Go over A, under B, over and around C. To return; go over B, over A, and return by the same route to X. Go around X, and repeat the operation. Each trip up and each trip down counts as one warp end, so now you have warped two ends. For a warp of 200 ends, 100 round trips will be made.

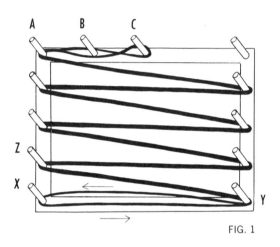

FIG. 1

To keep track of how many ends have been warped, tie groups of threads together with string. Each group should have the same number of ends as there are ends per inch, for easy counting by inches.

Striped warps are made the same way. Make the color change at Peg X, or C, according to the number of warp threads needed as indicated in the Warping Order. The warp thread is broken at the peg, and the next color tied to it, and warping continues.

Should you come to a knot in the yarn as you are warping, take the knot back to the last end peg, break and tie at the peg, discarding the knot. In this way your warp will be free of knots.

Tying the Warp   While the warp is still on the frame, secure the cross by tying, (Fig. 2).

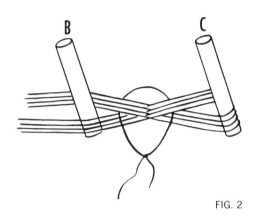

FIG. 2

Chaining the Warp   If you know how to crochet, this will be easy, as that is exactly what you do on a large scale. Put your hand through the warp at Peg X, keep it taut, and grasp the complete warp, and pull it through the loop. Repeat this operation, making a large, loose chain of the warp. The purpose of the chain is to shorten and prevent the warp from becoming tangled.

Leash Sticks   are now inserted at each side of the cross that was made on the warping frame. Tie the ends of the sticks together about 1″ apart. Shoe strings make good ties for leash sticks, and are easily threaded through the end holes. The cross is now secure, and the string used to tie it is removed. (Fig. 3)

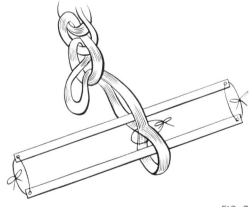

FIG. 3

Beaming A third stick, (a wooden dowel, or steel rod), is passed through the end loop of the warp chain. Spread the warp to its width on this rod, and attach the rod to the warp beam apron. (Fig. 4) It is good practice to spread the warp a bit wider on the back beam than its reed width. Less draw-in will occur during weaving.

Raddling A raddle is needed to keep the warp spread to its width during winding. These can be bought, or made by driving finishing nails ½″ apart in a ½″ × 1″ board as long as the loom is wide. The nails should extend about 1″ above the board. Tie or clamp the raddle to the loom, just back of the heddle frames. Into each of the ½″ spaces, place a number of warp threads equal to one half the number of ends per inch. In order for the warp to roll, it is absolutely neces-

sary that the threads are spread in the raddle in the exact order in which they are in the cross.

Rolling on the Warp This is much easier with a helper to wind the warp as you hold the warp at the front of the loom.

Tie the leash sticks to some part of the loom to keep them in place while winding the warp.

The warp is unchained as needed.

Wrapping paper, a bit wider than the warp, should be wound between every layer of warp.

Rolling should cease with any tug of the warp until the reason for it is found. Often all that is needed is to gently snap the warp while holding it out from the front beam.

At the end of rolling, cut and trim the end loops. Leave about 8″ in front of the first harness for threading.

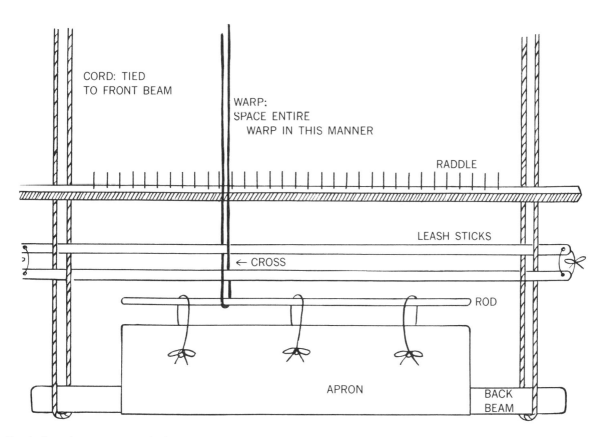

For clarity, only one warp yarn is shown.   FIG. 4

FACING THE BACK OF THE LOOM

Threading Looms come equipped with harnesses, (heddle frames), the number varying from 2, 4, 8, and more for multiple harness weaving.

A loom with two harnesses is known as a 2 harness loom, and only a web requiring two harnesses may be woven on it.

Most home weaving looms are 4 harness and will be discussed here, although the principle is the same for any number of harnesses.

The harness frames are arranged in the loom one after another. The order of numbering is sometimes reversed, but in this book the harness closest to the weaver at the front of the loom is to be harness number 1, and the one furthest away, harness number 4.

The frames hold heddles, usually made of steel or wire, but sometimes of string, having an eye in the center of each heddle. Through this eye the warp is threaded with a hook supplied with the loom.

To thread, push the heddles to the left except for a few on each frame. Grasp a group of warp ends in the left hand, the hook in the right hand with the few heddles between the hands. Thread from right to left in the sequence laid out in the pattern. With a little practice, you will find that the left hand assists in separating the warp threads, and keeping them in order for the heddles. The hook goes through the heddle eye, catches the thread, and pulls it through the eye. After threading a group, loosely loop together for safety, always checking to see that all is in order.

Unless otherwise stated, pull one warp thread through each eye, except selvage threads, which are threaded two to each heddle. "Double in the heddle," in the instructions, means that the complete warp is threaded double through the eyes. This pair will also be threaded in one dent in the reed.

Patterns give threading both in draft form, and by numbers.

Probably the beginner will find it easier to thread by numbers.

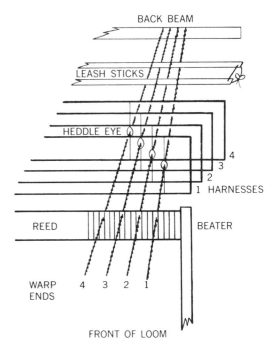

FIG. 5

Example: Thread 1, 2, 3, 4.

Thread the first warp end at the right through a heddle eye on harness 1, the second end through a heddle on harness 2, and through 3 and 4, and repeat.

Should threading be 3, 4, 3, 2, the first end is threaded through a heddle on harness 3, the second on harness 4, the third on harness 3, and the fourth end on harness 2. The longer threadings should be copied on paper and taped to the loom for easier reading.

To read from the threading draft, consider each black square a warp thread, and read from right to left in the direction of threading. The lowest horizontal row of squares represents harness 1, the top row is harness 4. Thread a warp end through the heddle on the harness indicated by the black square. (Fig. 5)

(12)

In some patterns a number below a section is the number of times this section is to be repeated before going to the next.

It is helpful to count off the heddles needed for a repeat of the pattern, even if only 4 heddles, (1, 2, 3, 4,) or several for a more intricate pattern. Thread these in their proper order, then count off the next repeat group for threading.

Denting If the beater with the reed has been removed for threading, place it in position.

The warp is now threaded through the spaces in the reed according to the pattern instructions.

To center the warp in the reed, find the middle of the reed, then measure a distance to the right equal to half the width of the warp, and begin denting at this point. Work from right to left, again holding the hook in the right hand.

12 dent which will give besides the 24 to the inch @ 2 per dent, 18 to the inch when dented 1 per dent, 2 per dent and repeated. If a third reed is included in the equipment, a 10 dent reed will be useful, especially for a mixed warp, denting the heavier yarns at 1 per dent, and the finer yarns @ 2 or 3 per dent.

After a group of 15 or 20 ends have passed through the reed, loop them together loosely for safety.

Tying Warp to Cloth Beam After all the warp ends have gone through the reed, tie them in groups onto the cloth beam rod as shown in Fig. 6.

It is best to tie the center knot group, then tie alternate sides until all the warp threads are secure.

To prepare the threads for tying, stroke them toward you until there are no

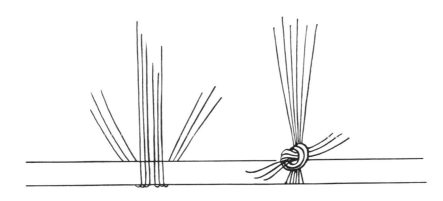

FIG. 6

Some patterns call for empty dents. Skip these dents according to the number stated. Uneven spacing is created in this way, which is effective in some weaves.

The size of the reed is not in relation to its length, but to how many spaces it has to the inch. Most American looms come with a 15 dent reed which will give 15 ends per inch, or 30 if the threads are doubled. The next most popular size is a

loose threads. The group should contain about one inch of threads in the reed for small widths, two inches for wider warps. This is one of the most important steps in warping as it creates the tension, and only a well-tensioned warp will weave into a smooth web. To test, run the back of the hand over the warp, if any looseness occurs, untie, and re-tie until uniform with the rest of the warp.

Tie-up for Floor Looms The floor pedals must be connected with lams which connect with the harness frames.

This connection is made by different methods on different looms, some looms having connecting metal rods, others have ropes, and some have ropes and hooks, but the principle is the same.

TIE-UP

6 5 4 3 2 1

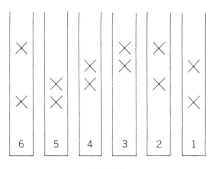

PEDALS

The tie-up is drawn on graph paper. The vertical row of squares represent one pedal, and each cross on it, a connection. Example:

In the first vertical row of squares, reading from the bottom up, a cross in squares 1 and 3 means that this pedal must be connected with lams connected to harnesses 1 and 3. Depressing the pedal will raise that part of the warp threaded through heddles on frames 1 and 3. Warp threaded on harness frames 2 and 4 will remain stationary. The space between is the shed through which the shuttle is passed, and weaving occurs. For the next weft shot, release pedal 1 and depress pedal 2.

Some small four harness floor looms come with only four foot pedals. Each of these pedals is tied permanently to a harness. To tread these pedals, follow table loom instructions holding one or more pedals down with the foot at one time.

Treadling For those patterns requiring only one shuttle, treadling order is given in numbers. For floor looms, the numbers refer to the pedals and for table looms, the lever combination to be depressed.

Weft stripe patterns requiring more than one shuttle list the different weft yarn colors, the number of shots of each, and the treadling order. Read from the top, down.

Example: 2 Red 1, 2
            4 White 1, 2 × 2

The number before the color is the number of shots to be woven, the numbers after the color is the treadling order. In the example, tread pedal 1, throw one shot of red, tread 2, and throw another shot of red yarn. Do the same with white yarn, but this time repeat again. Six picks (rows) will have been woven, 2 red, and 4 white.

Table loom treadling follows the same order, but each pedal number is converted to a combination of levers which is given for each pattern. Results will be the same on both looms.

If the order of treadling is written on paper and taped to the loom, it is more easily read, and can be checked off at intervals.

Table Loom Levers The tie-up operation is omitted for table looms. Hand levers are attached to harnesses permanently, and need never be changed. Depressing the first lever will raise harness frame 1 independently, and so on to the back lever and frame. In patterns calling for more than one harness to be raised at one time, two or three levers must be depressed at the same time.

Example: 1 + 3
            2 + 4

Levers 1 and 3 are depressed, raising warp threaded on harnesses 1 and 3. Warp threads on harness frames 2 and 4 remain down. The opening between the warp threads forms the shed through which the shuttle is passed.

(14)

The opposite will occur by depressing levers 2 and 4, forming another shed for weaving.

Requirements Where yarn amounts are given for one yard, this amount should be multiplied by the number of yards wanted, plus all allowances, as explained under **Warp** and **Weft.**

Many patterns, especially among the pillows and decorative fabrics, may be woven on the same warp with only the tie-up and treadling changed. These are listed when this is possible.

Equipment Looms come equipped with leash sticks, a threading hook, one reed, heddles, a winding crank and one or two shuttles with bobbins. Other pieces of equipment you will need are the previously mentioned raddle and warping frame, a spool rack, and bobbin winder. All of these may be ordered from the loom supply houses listed. A small hand-turned winder fills bobbins just as well as an electric one although not as speedily. A spool rack holds many tubes of yarn. For weaving using only one or two tubes, a shoe box clamped on its side to a table with a knitting needle stuck through from end to end will hold a tube of yarn as well as a rack. Other small items you probably already have: A pin cushion tied to the loom, a pair of scissors hanging from a hook, a handy tape measure, a pad and pencil, and some bright color-headed pins for marking off measurements on the web, are all helpful.

To Weave Start the weaving with heavy yarn or evenly torn rags. Weave until the spaces caused by tying the warp to the cloth beam rod are closed and all warp threads lie parallel. This weaving is cut off or raveled for fringe when the weaving is removed from the loom.

To begin the weaving, tread the first pedal according to the pattern treadling instructions which have been copied and taped to your loom. This action opens the V-shaped space in the warp called the "shed." Lightly slide the shuttle, with weft wound bobbin, through this space, leaving about 2". The shuttle can be entered from right or left, but for this book enter from the right. With the shuttle now in the left hand, grasp the beater exactly in the center and pull it forward and beat the weft into place.

To weave the next "shot" (row), release the pedal and tread the next according to the treadling instructions. This opens another shed. Bring the short piece on the right through this shed for about ½". In this same shed, enter ("throw") the second shot from left to right. Beat. Continue in this manner. After a few inches the protruding end is trimmed close.

For plain or tabby weave, only two pedals, tread alternately, are required. For pattern weaving you may use up to six pedals on a four harness loom. Use either foot or both feet for long treadlings, whichever seems the most natural and convenient.

Table loom weavers will press levers to open sheds and weave the same as on floor looms.

Learn to control the "beat," light for sheer fabrics and quick and sharp for heavy fabrics and rugs.

To change wefts, fasten as in the beginning, enter the new weft and fasten in the next shed.

Roll the "web" (weaving) forward after about every 2" or so. It must not be rolled too close to the front beam so as to leave room for the beater action.

When enough has been woven, wind forward around the cloth beam.

Rolling Forward Better weaving will result if the warp is wound forward often, and at short distances each time. The action of the beater is different on a web close to the breast beam than on one close to the beater. Good weavers move the warp forward about every 2″ of weaving.

Cloth Beam It is well to pad the cloth beam with heavy paper before rolling the web onto it. The paper will cover the ropes and tie-in knots, and prevent these from pressing into the weaving. If the warp is a heavy one, the knots may even cause uneven tension, so pad well at the beginning of rolling.

Looms There is no "best loom" for everyone. The loom must fit your needs and space. A study of loom catalogues will help in selection. The beginner will find it a great help to buy a loom which comes supplied with a book of instructions, not only on the loom and its parts, but how to warp and weave on that particular loom. Much weaving can be done on a two harness table loom, but it will soon be outgrown, and it is best to buy a four harness loom, and as wide as space permits. A 36″ width will weave everything except spreads and curtains, which may be woven in panels or in double-width. Whatever loom is on hand or purchased, should be kept oiled. There are few more irritating sounds than a squeaky loom, and a few drops of oil will make it much easier to operate, and increase pleasure in weaving.

Entering New Weft When it is necessary to enter a new weft, the join must be at the selvage side, never in the middle of the web. It is best to enter this new weft in the same shed as the old. To do this, enter the old thread for one inch at selvage side and bring it up through the warp to the top of the web. (Waste will occur, but it is unavoidable). Enter the new weft in the same shed, and in the same direction as the old thread, leaving a short end above the web at the selvage side. The old and the new weft now overlap about 1″, with the two ends lying on the surface of the web. Continue weaving. The two ends are cut off close to the fabric before rolling forward. When joining heavy plied yarns such as rug filler, untwist the end of the old, and stagger the single plys between warp threads. Untwist, and overlap the new weft in the same way, adjusting each until flat and neat. After a hard beat, a few more shots and clipping the ends, the join can scarcely be seen.

If the new weft is of another color, the old weft is cut a few inches beyond selvage side, caught around the last selvage end and brought back into the same shed for one inch, bringing the end to the web's surface. Change sheds, enter the new weft of a different color in this shed, leaving a 1½″ "tail," which is woven into the next shed for about one inch, the end is brought to the top of the web. After a bit of weaving, snip the two ends.

Repairing Broken Warp Threads A two yard length of warp thread identical to the one broken is threaded through the empty heddle and dent. The front end is wrapped around a pin in the web, and after a few inches of weaving it must be darned down beside the old warp thread for about two inches. To tension the repair thread while weaving, hang a weight on the other end at the back of the loom. The weight may be anything from a clothespin to a tube of yarn, depending on the established tension of the warp. Test the repair thread with the back of the hand until it conforms to the rest of the warp tension. Weave until the old broken end is long enough to be brought forward through heddle and dent, wrapped around a pin in the web, leaving the repair yarn as it is. Weave two inches. Remove what is left of the repair yarn and snip the pin-wrapped yarn. If the break occurs while weaving articles to be cut apart, such as mats and pillows, or comes at nearly the end of yardage, the last step is omitted.

If warp and weft are identical yarns, the old thread and the repair thread need not be pin-wrapped and darned. Simply cross the two in the open shed, laying each in opposite directions for about two inches.

For a Clean Shed Check all sheds before weaving. If crossed warp threads are seen, the mistake is usually in the reeding. To remedy, untie, and pull out crossed ends from the reed, line them up from heddles to reed, then redent them correctly.

The Beater The beater, as its name implies, beats the weft into place. The force with which the beater is brought forward is determined by the type of web being woven. For rugs the beat must be hard, even two sharp beats are required for some rugs. For sheer fabrics, such as casement cloth, the beater is brought gently forward, just placing the weft. For upholsteries the beat is firm and so on.

The beater holds the reed which in turn keeps the warp threads separated and in position.

The beater should always be brought forward with the hand exactly in the middle of it, otherwise the angle at which it beats will cause the weaving to build up more on one side than the other. Counting the rows of weft per inch as weaving progresses, always keeping them the same, will produce uniform weaving.

Heddles Looms usually come equipped with thirty heddles per inch. At this rate, a 20", four harness loom would have a total of 600 heddles, or 150 heddles on each heddle frame. If the weaving width is to be 20" @ 15 ends per inch, a total of only 300 heddles are needed, or 75 on each of the four frames. There will be twice as many heddles as are needed on each frame. There is not room to push these to the sides when weaving loom capacity. Rather than remove the unneeded heddles, for each heddle threaded, leave the next heddle empty. The empty heddles will not interfere with weaving.

Some pattern drafts call for more heddles on some heddle frames than others, then heddles must be switched from one frame to another. A pair of oversize blanket safety-pins is good equipment for this. Simply thread the pins through the top and bottom of the heddles along the bars, snap the pins closed, remove, and make the change.

Bobbins To wind bobbins, start at one end, and wind cone-shaped, pointing inward. When the bobbin is filled at one end, fill the opposite end in the same way. The third step is to fill the center until it is as high as the sides. A few extra turns of the winder are made so that the bobbin holds all that is possible, and can still turn freely in the shuttle.

Insert the bobbin in the shuttle with the yarn coming from underneath. It seems to roll better, and there are technical reasons for it. Yarns are twisted in different directions, and by many methods, the study of which is vast and need not concern the homeweaver. Knowing the condition exists, and that trouble can be avoided by always having yarns pull from underneath, is sufficient. This practice should also be carried out on the spool rack.

Some single ply homespun-type woolen yarns twist and curl as they come from the bobbin. Winding the next day's bobbins the night before will help to straighten them. Bobbins should not be left too long, as in time the winding will lessen the elasticity of the yarn.

Measuring To measure on the loom, use two large pins. Insert one in the selvage side to mark the amount woven, and note the figure on a pad. Before this marker is rolled over the front beam, take a second pin, and measure up from the first pin. Add this amount to the first figure, and proceed in this way to the end of weaving. Measuring can be done with one pin, but there is less chance of losing one's place with two pins, always leaving the first in until the second is in place.

To measure yardage, use a length of contrasting carpet warp 3″ longer than the length of weaving is to be. Wrap the first 3″ around a pin at the beginning of the web. Do not remove this pin. Roll the remaining thread around a tube or bobbin, and let it hang from the front. As weaving progresses, pin this thread to the web, and roll it up along with the woven fabric. The end of the thread will be the end of weaving. If a check as you weave is wanted, a bit of chalk on the string marking the yards will give the information which can be noted on a pad. The length of the measuring string is determined by the yards wanted, plus take-up, and all other necessary allowances.

Another marking help is to mark off each woven yard on the loom with a piece of thread tied selvage side. When the web is removed from the loom, an accurate check of how many inches were lost in take-up per yard can be made instead of figuring from the whole length. Leave these strings in through finishing, be it pressing, or scouring, for a final check. This is valuable information for further weaving projects.

Records Other information you will want to keep, besides those under headings on the instruction pages, will be width shrinkage, type of finishing, source, and cost of materials, dates, and weaving hours. To the weaving hours, add warping time, time spent dressing the loom, and finishing time, to be ready with an accurate answer to that inevitable question: "How long did it take?"

Samples Always put a bit more warp on than called for. Unpleasant take-up "surprises" will be avoided, and it will give a little extra at the end for sampling. The width of the samples can be made narrower than the weaving by removing warp threads from either side. A sample of what has been woven will be wanted for a record. After that, any yarn and treadling may be tried. Some of the most interesting fabrics have been developed from end-of-warp sample weaving.

Twill Weave Twill should always be woven at a 45° angle. Three things must be considered and their influence on each other to arrive at this slant; the size of the yarn, the set and the beat. Of these, the beat has the greatest influence on the slant.

Traditionally the direction of the slant in the U.S. is up from left to right and woven in reverse in most other countries. Both slants are used in this book. Should you prefer the opposite slant to the one given, simply reverse the order of treadling. Example: Given treading 1, 2, 3, 4. To reverse the direction of the slant, tread 4, 3, 2, 1.

Yardage Table for Standard Cotton Yarns Used in the Patterns

Size	Yards per lb.
5/2	2100
8/2	3360
10/2	4200
12/4	2520
16/2	6720
20/2	8400
24/3	6720
Pearl 3	1260
Pearl 5	2100
8/4 Carpet warp	800 Yds. per ½ lb.
4/4 Carpet warp	400 Yds. per ½ lb.

UPHOLSTERY

Upholstery fabrics, obviously, must be of a firm weave with long floats avoided. They should, however, be pliable enough to fit around various parts of furniture. A cotton warp is usually best because of its slightly elastic character which will tend to give a fabric this quality. There is an old saying that "wool wears itself clean," and it seems to be true. Upholsteries woven with a wool weft do stay clean much longer. When wool is not suited to the type of furniture the fabric is to cover, cottons and synthetics are used. Even if synthetics are not liked for many other handwoven fabrics, they do work well in upholsteries, and are long wearing.

Since power-loomed upholstery always comes in 50" to 54" widths, many handweavers believe they cannot weave them because of narrower looms. Decorators who use handwoven fabrics usually specify a 32" finished upholstery width. They feel this is the most satisfactory width for all pieces, including sofas. True, more yardage must be woven, but it can be woven on a 36" loom. To be safe, the warp should be set 35" or even 36" in the reed. The 32" fabric is used with selvages running parallel to the length of the sofa. This gives a seamless back, back of back, and in the case of a single long cushion, it too is seamless. Since most seats do not exceed 24" in depth, the 32" width is ample for the top, plus the boxing. If self-welting is used, extra must be woven for it.

Patterns that are especially adaptable to the 32" width are shown on pages 26, 29, and 30. The weft stripe will run from front to back on the seat cushion, and vertically on the back.

Upholstery can be woven on table looms as well as floor looms, but of course in narrower widths, for benches, stools and chair seats.

Warp stripe patterns are usually used with the stripes running vertically, although these too may be used in the same way as weft stripe patterns on modern sofas or chairs.

In the case of a warp used for both curtains and upholstery, the curtains will determine the width and be woven off first, warp removed to upholstery width, and then woven.

Upholstery fabric needs a firm, sharp beat.

The only finish needed is a good steam pressing.

Some of the closely woven tabby weaves make suitable fabrics for slip covers. Maintenance determines the finish of such fabrics. If to be dry cleaned, a steam pressing is sufficient, but if the cover is to be washed, wash-test a sample for shrinkage. It may be advisable to wash the fabric before cutting.

UPHOLSTERY

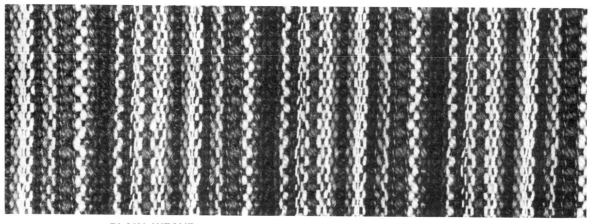

PLAIN WEAVE

WARP:
Pearl 3 cotton
    Black
    Taupe
    Linen color
Carpet warp 8/4
    Beige
Cotton novelty, size 1
    Black
Cotton 10/2
    Linen color
Cotton 12/4
    Olive
Cotton 24/3
    Natural
Merc. cotton 20/3
    Brown
    White
Worsted 10/2
    Dk. red
    Black
    Sand
    Grey
12 cut wool
    Taffy

THREADING   TIE-UP

2 1

WEFT: Black cotton ratine @ 1450 yds. per lb.
WARP ENDS: 792
ENDS PER INCH: 22
REED: 12
WIDTH IN REED: 36″
DENTING: 2 per dent except pearl cotton @ 1 per dent
THREAD: 1, 2, 3, 4 in same order as warping order
One to heddle except red @ 2 per heddle
TREADLING: 1, 2
TABLE LOOMS:
Levers 1 + 3
       2 + 4
This fabric is also suitable for drapes.

WARPING ORDER: 44 end repeat = 2″

2 red (2 to heddle)
2 brown
2 taffy
1 olive
1 brown
2 black worsted
2 linen color 10/2 cotton
2 natural 24/3 cotton
1 white 20/3 cotton

1 sand worsted
2 olive
1 black pearl
2 olive
2 linen color 10/2 cotton
1 taffy
1 beige carpet warp
1 beige carpet warp
1 taffy

2 natural 24/3 cotton
2 black worsted
1 taupe pearl
1 grey worsted
1 black worsted
1 black novelty
1 black worsted
2 olive
2 linen color pearl
2 brown

CHAIR SEAT FABRIC

4 harness, 4 pedal

WARP: 4 ply cotton @ 2700 yds. per lb.
Coral pink or any light color

WEFT: Black all purpose rayon @ 100 yds. per 2 oz.

WARP ENDS: 360

ENDS PER INCH: 18

REED: 9

WIDTH IN REED: 20″

DENTING: 2 per dent

THREAD: One to heddle
4, 3, 4, 3, 2, 3, 4, 3, 4
1, 2, 1, 2, 3, 2, 1, 2, 1

TREADLING: 1, 2, 3, 2, 1, 4

TABLE LOOMS:
For pedal 1 use levers 1 + 2
For pedal 2 use levers 1 + 4
For pedal 3 use levers 3 + 4
For pedal 4 use levers 2 + 3

REQUIREMENTS: For 1 yd.
Warp, 360 yds.
Weft, 400 yds.

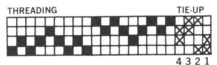

THREADING   TIE-UP

4 3 2 1

UPHOLSTERY

4 harness, 3 pedal

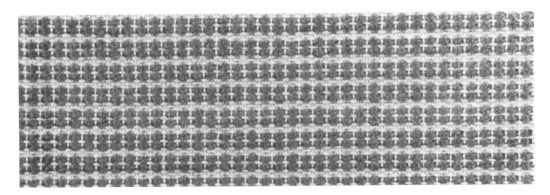

WARP: Unmercerized 16/2 beige cotton

WEFT: Beige 3 ply crimp set nylon
Lt. brown 3 strand, 2 ply persian wool

WARP ENDS: 864

ENDS PER INCH: 24

REED: 12

WIDTH IN REED: 36″

DENTING: 2 per dent

THREAD: One to heddle 1, 2, 3, 4

TREADLING:
3 beige 1, 2, 1
1 brown 3
1 beige 1
1 brown 3 Repeat

THREADING TIE-UP

3 2 1

TABLE LOOMS:
For pedal 1 use levers 2 + 4
For pedal 2 use levers 1 + 3
For pedal 3 use lever 1

REQUIREMENTS: For 1 yd.
Warp, 864 yds.
Nylon, 720 yds.
Wool, 360 yds.

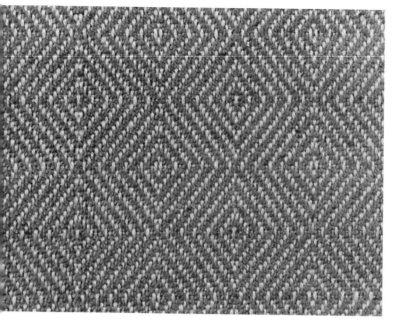

4 harness, 4 pedal

WARP: Natural 20/2 ramie @ 3,000 yds. per lb.

WEFT: Linen color mercerized pearl 3 cotton @ 1260 yds. per lb.

WARP ENDS: 864

ENDS PER INCH: 24

REED: 12

WIDTH IN REED: 36″

DENTING: 2 per dent

THREAD: 1 per heddle, end on H1
4, 3, 2, 1, ×3
4, 3, 2
1, 2, 3, 4, ×3
1, 2, 3

TREADLING:
4, 3, 2, 1, ×3
4, 3, 2
1, 2, 3, 4, ×3
1, 2, 3

TABLE LOOMS:
For pedal 1 use levers 2 + 3
For pedal 2 use levers 3 + 4
For pedal 3 use levers 1 + 4
For pedal 4 use levers 1 + 2

REQUIREMENTS: For 1 yd.
Ramie warp, 864 yds.
Pearl weft, 864 yds.

4 harness, 6 pedal

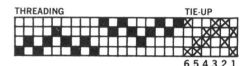

6 5 4 3 2 1

WARP: 4 ply cotton @ 2700 yds. per lb.
Lt. green or any light color

WEFT: Viscose and jute twist @ 1200 yds.
Cotton, same as warp for tabby

WARP ENDS: 648

ENDS PER INCH: 18

REED: 9

WIDTH IN REED: 36″

DENTING: 2 per dent

THREAD: One per heddle
4, 3, 4, 3, 2, 3, 4, 3, 4,
1, 2, 1, 2, 3, 2, 1, 2, 1

TREADLING: One shot tabby 1, 2 between every pattern shot
Viscose
3 × 2, 4
3 × 2, 6
5 × 2, 4
5 × 2, 6

TABLE LOOMS:
For pedal 1 use levers 1 + 3
For pedal 2 use levers 2 + 4
For pedal 3 use levers 3 + 4
For pedal 4 use levers 2 + 3
For pedal 5 use levers 1 + 2
For pedal 6 use levers 1 + 4

REQUIREMENTS: For 1 yd.
Cotton, warp and weft, 1368 yds.
Viscose, 720 yds.

UPHOLSTERY

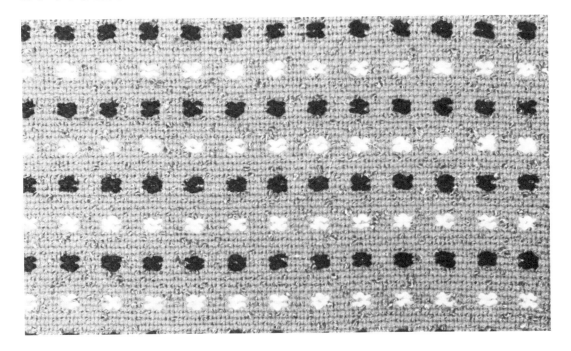

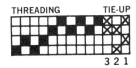

THREADING   TIE-UP

3 2 1

MONK'S BELT WEAVE

WARP: Tobacco color 4 ply cotton @ 2700 yds. per lb.

WEFT: Cotton same as warp ⎫ Wound
      Antique gold color rayon ⎬ together
      bouclé ⎭
      Cotton ratine @ 1450 yds. per lb.
        Black
        Natural

WARP ENDS: 720

ENDS PER INCH: 20

REED: 10

WIDTH IN REED: 36"

DENTING: 2 per dent

THREAD: One per heddle
4, 3, 4, 3, 4, 3
2, 1, 2, 1

TREADLING:
5 ground 1, 2, 1, 2, 1
1 natural 3
1 ground 2
1 natural 3
5 ground 1, 2, 1, 2, 1
1 black 3
1 ground 2
1 black 3
Repeat

TABLE LOOMS:
For pedal 1 use levers 2 + 4
For pedal 2 use levers 1 + 3
For pedal 3 use levers 3 + 4

REQUIREMENTS: For 1 yd.
4 ply cotton, warp and weft, 1440 yds.
Bouclé, 720 yds.
Black ratine, 75 yds.
Natural ratine, 75 yds.
May be woven on the same warp as on page 25.

(23)

THREADING TIE-UP

2 1

PLAIN WEAVE

WARP:

Navy 8/2 cotton

Purple rayon bouclé

Olive 5/2 cotton

Fuchsia wool spun rayon

Green variegated 2 ply soft spun rayon ratine

WEFT: Above

Purple rayon bouclé

Green variegated ratine

Black pearl 3 cotton

Below

Black pearl 3 cotton

WARP ENDS: 576

ENDS PER INCH: 16

REED: 8

WIDTH IN REED: 36″

DENTING: 2 per dent

THREAD: 1, 2, 3, 4 exactly in warping order

WARPING ORDER: One to heddle

1 navy

1 purple

1 olive

1 fuchsia

1 green

Substitute navy for green in last repeat at left selvage.

TREADLING: Above

1 green 1

1 purple 2

1 black 1

1 green 2

1 purple 1

1 black 2

Repeat

Below

Black pearl 1, 2

TABLE LOOMS:

For pedal 1 use levers 1 + 3

For pedal 2 use levers 2 + 4

Fabrics also suitable for unlined drapes.

UPHOLSTERY

4 harness, 3 pedal

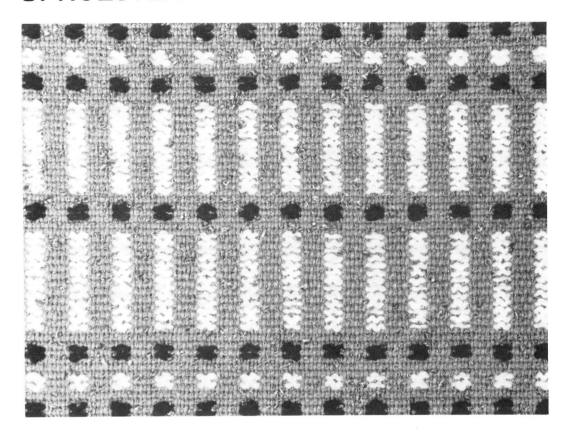

THREADING   TIE-UP

3 2 1

MONK'S BELT WEAVE

WARP: Tobacco color 4 ply cotton @ 2700
   yds. per lb.

WEFT: Cotton same as warp   ⎫ Wound
     Antique gold color rayon ⎬ together
       bouclé   ⎭
     Cotton ratine @ 1450 yds. per lb.
       Black
       White

WARP ENDS: 720

ENDS PER INCH: 20

REED: 10

WIDTH IN REED: 36″

DENTING: 2 per dent

THREAD: One per heddle
4, 3, 4, 3, 4, 3
2, 1, 2, 1

REQUIREMENTS: For 1 yd.
4 ply cotton, warp and weft, 1440 yds.
Bouclé, 720 yds.
Black ratine, 75 yds.
Natural ratine, 340 yds.
May be woven on the same warp as
   on page 23.

(25)

TREADLING:

Ground 1, 2, 1
Natural 3 ⎫
Ground 2 ⎪
Natural 3 ⎬ ×6
Ground 1 ⎭
Natural 3
Ground 2, 1, 2
Black 3
Ground 1
Black 3
Ground 2, 1, 2
Natural 3
Ground 1
Natural 3
Ground 2, 1, 2
Black 3

Ground 1
Black 3
Ground 2, 1, 2
Natural 3 ⎫
Ground 1 ⎪
Natural 3 ⎬ ×6
Ground 2 ⎭
Natural 3
Ground 1, 2, 1
Black 3
Ground 2
Black 3

TABLE LOOMS:
For pedal 1 use levers 2 + 4
For pedal 2 use levers 1 + 3
For pedal 3 use levers 3 + 4

UPHOLSTERY

4 harness, 4 pedal

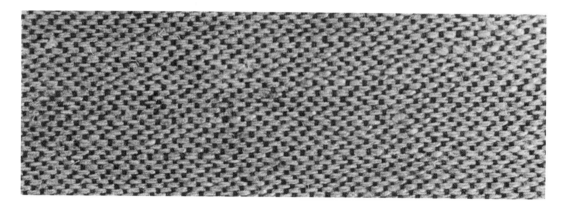

BROKEN TWILL

WARP: Black 4 ply cotton @ 2700 yds. per lb.

WEFT: Peacock 4 ply cotton ⎫ Wound
Peacock slub linen ⎭ together

WARP ENDS: 720

ENDS PER INCH: 20

REED: 10

WIDTH IN REED: 36"

DENTING: 2 per dent

THREAD: 1 per heddle 1, 2, 3, 4

THREADING   TIE-UP

4 3 2 1

TREADLING: 1, 2, 3, 4

TABLE LOOMS:
For pedal 1 use lever 4
For pedal 2 use lever 3
For pedal 3 use lever 1
For pedal 4 use lever 2

REQUIREMENTS: For 1 yd.
Black cotton warp, 720 yds.
Peacock cotton, 750 yds.
Peacock linen, 750 yds.

UPHOLSTERY

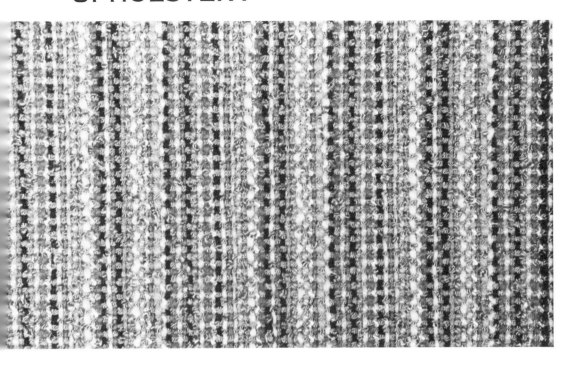

PLAIN WEAVE

WARP:
Cotton 4/4
    Mustard
    Natural
Cotton 8/4
    Orange
    Black
    Beige
    Natural
Cotton 12/4
    Peacock
    Black
Pearl 3 cotton
    Linen color
    Taupe
    Lt. yellow
    Buff
Cotton ratine
    Rust
    Natural
Rayon ratine
    White
Rayon bouclé
    Old gold color

THREADING TIE-UP

2 1

WEFT: Rayon bouclé @ 1700 yds. per lb.
    Old gold color, doubled

WARP ENDS: 540

ENDS PER INCH: 15

REED: 10

WIDTH IN REED: 36″

DENTING: One per dent except 2 per dent
    where indicated

THREAD: 1, 2, 3, 4 in same order as warp-
    ing order. One end of each color.
Single in the heddle

TREADLING: Doubled weft 1, 2

TABLE LOOMS:
Levers 1 + 3
      2 + 4

(27)

WARPING ORDER:
30 end repeat = 2"
1 dent mustard
1 dent { peacock
         { white rayon ratine
1 dent { linen color pearl
         { natural cotton ratine
1 dent taupe pearl
1 dent orange
1 dent { black 12/4
         { peacock
1 dent natural 4/4
1 dent { black 8/4
         { rust
1 dent { white rayon ratine
         { natural 4/4

1 dent { gold bouclé
         { linen color pearl
1 dent { beige
         { peacock
1 dent natural 8/4
1 dent black 8/4
1 dent { white rayon ratine
         { rust
1 dent lt. yellow pearl
1 dent taupe pearl
1 dent { black 12/4
         { peacock
1 dent buff pearl
1 dent { rust
         { black 12/4
1 dent natural cotton ratine

UPHOLSTERY

4 harness, 4 pedal

THREADING TIE-UP

4 3 2 1

BROKEN TWILL

WARP: Unmercerized lt. grey cotton 16/2
or 20/2
WEFT: 2 yellow heather 7/1 wool
Natural slub linen } Wound together
WARP ENDS: 864
ENDS PER INCH: 24
REED: 12
WIDTH IN REED: 36"
DENTING: 2 per dent
THREAD: 1 per heddle 1, 2, 3, 4

TREADLING: 1, 2, 3, 4
TABLE LOOMS:
For pedal 1 use lever 4
For pedal 2 use lever 3
For pedal 3 use lever 1
For pedal 4 use lever 2
REQUIREMENTS: For 1 yd.
Grey cotton warp, 864 yds.
Yellow wool, 1750 yds.
Slub linen, 875 yds.
May be woven on the same warp as on
page 29.

UPHOLSTERY

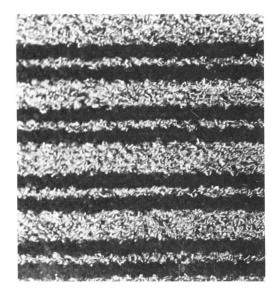

BROKEN TWILL

WARP: Unmercerized lt. grey cotton 16/2 or 20/2

WEFT: Antique gold color rayon bouclé @ 1700 yds. per lb.
   Dark green 12 cut cotton chenille @ 1200 yds. per lb.

WARP ENDS: 864

ENDS PER INCH: 24

REED: 12

WIDTH IN REED: 36"

DENTING: 2 per dent

THREAD: 1 per heddle 1, 2, 3, 4

THREADING TIE-UP

4 3 2 1

REQUIREMENTS: For 1 yd.
Grey cotton warp 864 yds.
Bouclé, 875 yds.
Chenille, 450 yds.

TREADLING:
12 bouclé 1, 2, 3, 4 ×3
 4 chenille 1, 2, 3, 4
 4 bouclé 1, 2, 3, 4
 4 chenille 1, 2, 3, 4
For a solid color upholstery:
   Tread bouclé 1, 2, 3, 4

TABLE LOOMS:
For pedal 1 use lever 4
For pedal 2 use lever 3
For pedal 3 use lever 1
For pedal 4 use lever 2

TWILL AND REVERSED TWILL

WARP: Natural 8/2 cotton @ 3360 yds. per lb.

WEFT: Viscose—jute twist @ 1200 yds. per lb.

WARP ENDS: 864

ENDS PER INCH: 24

REED: 12

WIDTH IN REED: 36"

THREADING TIE-UP

4 3 2 1

DENTING: 2 per dent

THREAD: One per heddle 1, 2, 3, 4

TREADLING:
1, 2, 3, 4 ×3
1, 2, 3
4, 3, 2, 1 ×3
4, 3, 2

TABLE LOOMS:
For pedal 1 use levers 3 + 4
For pedal 2 use levers 2 + 3
For pedal 3 use levers 1 + 2
For pedal 4 use levers 1 + 4

REQUIREMENTS: For 1 yd.
Warp, 864 yds.
Weft, 800 yds.

CHAIR SEAT FABRICS

BROKEN TWILL

WARP: Unmercerized lt. grey cotton 16/2 or 20/2

WEFT: 4/4 cotton @ 400 yds. per 8 oz.
Natural
Mustard
Lt. grey
Dk. green

WARP ENDS: 480

ENDS PER INCH: 24

REED: 12

WIDTH IN REED: 20"

DENTING: 2 per dent

THREAD: One to heddle 1, 2, 3, 4

TREADLING: 1, 2, 3, 4
8 mustard
2 natural
4 green
4 natural
2 grey
4 natural

TABLE LOOMS:
For pedal 1 use lever 4
For pedal 2 use lever 3
For pedal 3 use lever 1
For pedal 4 use lever 2

REQUIREMENTS: For 1 yd.
Warp, 480 yds.
Natural, 180 yds.
Mustard, 144 yds.
Green, 72 yds.
Grey, 36 yds.

THREADING TIE-UP

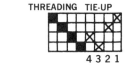

4 3 2 1

WEFT: Persian 3 strand, 2 ply wool yarn
Beige
Tan
Lt. brown

TREADLING: 1, 2, 3, 4
2 beige
2 tan
2 brown
3 beige
3 tan
3 brown
4 beige
4 tan
4 brown
5 beige
5 tan
5 brown
6 beige
6 tan
7 brown **(center)**
Repeat in reverse, 6 tan etc.

REQUIREMENTS: For 1 yd.
Warp, 480 yds.
Beige, 170 yds.
Tan, 170 yds.
Brown, 170 yds.

UPHOLSTERY

4 harness, 2 pedal

THREADING   TIE-UP

2 1

PLAIN WEAVE

WARP:
Pearl 3 cotton
    Nutaupe
    Brown
    Emerald
    Maroon
Cotton 8/4
    Beige
    Dk. green
Cotton 4/4
    Orange
    Dk. green
Cotton 5/2
    Olive
Cotton 12/4 or 10/3
    Chartreuse
    Emerald
    Black
    Navy
Cotton ratine
    Chartreuse
    Black
    Rust
Rayon bouclé
    Old gold color
    Chartreuse
Dk. orange 2 ply rayon

WEFT:
Olive 5/2 cotton, doubled
Brown cotton knot
Old gold color rayon bouclé, doubled
Dk. brown Canadian mop yarn

WARP ENDS: 576

ENDS PER INCH: 16

REED: 12

WIDTH IN REED: 36″

THREAD: 1, 2, 3, 4 in same order as warping order
32 end repeat = 2″

TREADLING:
Bouclé, doubled, 1
Olive, doubled, 2
Knot 1
Olive, doubled, 2
Brown 1
Bouclé, doubled, 2
Olive, doubled, 1
Knot 2
Olive, doubled, 1
Brown 2
Repeat

TABLE LOOMS:
For pedal 1 use levers 1 + 3
For pedal 2 use levers 2 + 4

WARPING ORDER: Numbers indicate no. of ends of a color and ends per dent except where indicated

1 nutaupe pearl
1 chartreuse cotton ratine
2 navy—1 heddle
1 orange rayon
1 beige
2 chartreuse 12/4—1 heddle
1 maroon pearl
1 black ratine
1 orange 4/4
1 chartreuse 12/4 ⎫
1 emerald 12/4 ⎬ 1 dent

1 olive
1 emerald pearl
2 navy—1 heddle
2 old gold bouclé—1 heddle
1 dk. green 8/4
1 orange 4/4
1 brown pearl
1 beige
1 nutaupe pearl
1 dk. green 4/4
2 chartreuse bouclé—1 heddle
2 navy—1 heddle
1 rust
2 black 12/4

SLIP COVER FABRIC

4 harness, 2 pedal

PLAIN WEAVE

WARP: 4 ply cotton @ 2700 yds. per lb.
Lt. green
Peacock

WEFT: Blue-green 20/1 linen @ 6000 yds. per lb.

WARP ENDS: 900

ENDS PER INCH: 20

REED: 10

WIDTH IN REED: 45″

DENTING: 2 per dent

THREAD: Single in heddle 1, 2, 3, 4
Thread whichever color comes up. Colors will alternate at times. Occasionally two greens or two blues will be heddled side by side. There will be no exact repeat in the width.

THREADING TIE-UP

2 1

WARPING ORDER: One end of each color together.

TREADLING: 1, 2

TABLE LOOMS:
Levers: 1 + 3
2 + 4

REQUIREMENTS: For 1 yd.
Lt. green, 450 yds.
Peacock, 450 yds.
Linen weft, 990 yds.

UPHOLSTERY

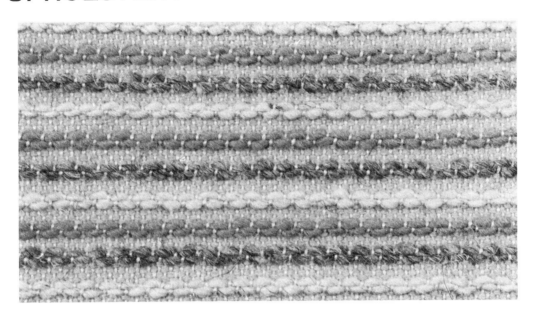

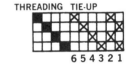

6 5 4 3 2 1

WARP: Natural Swedish 22/2 cottolin, 54% cotton, 46% linen @ 3250 yds. per lb.

WEFT: Beige 3 ply crimp set nylon
      Swedish cowhair
         Natural
         Med. grey
         Yellow

WARP ENDS: 540

ENDS PER INCH: 15

REED: 15

WIDTH IN REED: 36″

DENTING: 1 per dent

THREAD: One to heddle 1, 2, 3, 4

TREADLING:
Nylon 1, 2, 1, 2
Natural 3, 4
Nylon 1, 2, 1, 2
Grey 5, 6
Nylon 1, 2, 1, 2
Yellow 3, 4
Nylon 1, 2, 1, 2
Natural 5, 6
Nylon 1, 2, 1, 2
Grey 3, 4
Nylon 1, 2, 1, 2
Yellow 5, 6

TABLE LOOMS:
For pedal 1 use levers 1 + 3
For pedal 2 use levers 2 + 4
For pedal 3 use lever 1
For pedal 4 use lever 2
For pedal 5 use lever 3
For pedal 6 use lever 4

REQUIREMENTS: For 1 yd.
Warp, 540 yds.
Nylon, 490 yds.
Natural, 90 yds.
Med. grey, 90 yds.
Yellow, 90 yds.

UPHOLSTERY

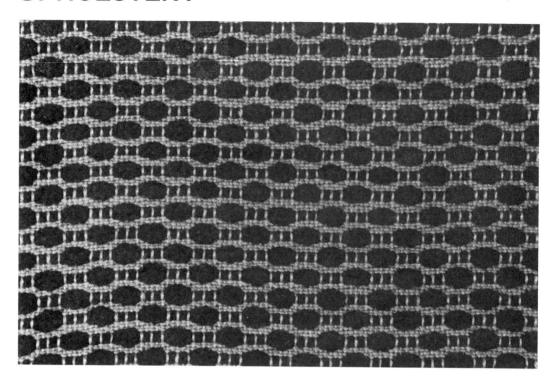

THREADING   TIE-UP

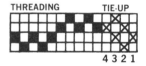

4 3 2 1

WARP: Peacock 4 ply cotton @ 2700 yds. per lb.

WEFT: Peacock same as warp
    Black cotton ratine @ 1450 yds.
      4 threads ratine wound
      together, used as one.

WARP ENDS: 675

ENDS PER INCH: 15

REED: 15

WIDTH IN REED: 45″

DENTING: 1 per dent

THREAD: One to heddle
3, 4, 3, 4, 3
2, 1, 2, 1, 2

TREADLING:
Peacock 2, 3, 2, 3
Ratine 4
Peacock 3, 2, 3, 2
Ratine 1

TABLE LOOMS:
For pedal 1 use lever 2
For pedal 2 use levers 1 + 3
For pedal 3 use levers 2 + 4
For pedal 4 use lever 3

REQUIREMENTS: For 1 yd.
Peacock cotton, warp and weft, 1575 yds.
Black ratine, 900 yds.
Pillows and curtains may be woven on this warp. Pillows: Substitute bright color wool yarn for ratine. Curtain: See page 36.

CURTAINS

Curtains take so little time and materials that they are a joy to weave, and so satisfying to use. There is nothing quite like sunlight through a handwoven curtain to give a room charm.

Curtains are made in many weights from the sheerest of casement cloth to heavy draperies, but they all must have the ability to fall in soft folds.

Open weaves and long floats are permissible because the fabric is not to be worn, sat or walked upon, with virtually no wearing qualities needed.

Since they are sun-exposed, they must be woven of only the best quality yarns, and in the case of color, only sunfast, vat-dyed yarns will do.

Many patterns use the same weft yarn as warp yarn. If two weights are used, it is advisable to use the heavier of the two for the warp to give better hanging quality.

For most curtains a light beat is required, and in some cases, the weft is only just placed by the beater.

When pairs of curtains are woven with weft stripes either in contrasting colors or in self-color, or even formed by beating, a guide should be used so that bands will tally and all panels will be the same length. After the band pattern has been established to the weaver's liking, be it 2" or 18", make a ruler of this band. Heavy white paper or a discarded white window shade cut in 1" wide strips makes a good ruler. Put the strip on the woven band under tension on the loom and indicate number of color changes, picks, treadling order, and any information that will help the weaving. A bit of crayon on color sections is a help. Make this exact, then use it for all bands, and your panels will be uniform. Use these custom-made rulers for place mats, bands in skirts, and any fabric where a weft striped band appears more than once.

If care is taken with the selvages, side seams are unnecessary for some curtains, and the general effect is more pleasing, with the selvages becoming part of the design.

Generous allowance should be made for curtain fullness. Twice the width to be spanned and even three times for sheer curtains should be woven.

The weaver with a narrow loom can weave curtains of any width by whip-stitching panels of as little as twelve inches together. If well planned, the seams may even become a part of the design.

Curtains should be made up with maintenance plans in mind. Except for the lace weaves, most curtains need only to be steam-pressed before using. If they are to be washed later, shrinkage will occur, and generous hems, even double hems, will give allowance for adjusting length.

Probably no other handweaving can provide so much warmth and relief from the materials of modern interiors as curtains. Great expanses of glass, softened by the graceful folds of casement cloth or drapes, unify the room as nothing else can.

CASEMENT CLOTH   CURTAIN

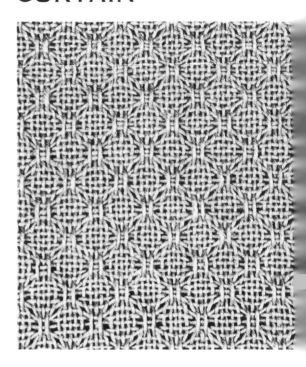

6 harness, 6 pedal   **4 harness, 4 pedal**

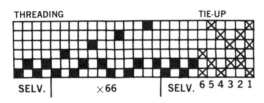

THREADING   TIE-UP

SELV. | ×66 | SELV.   6 5 4 3 2 1

DIAGONAL LACE WEAVE

WARP: Natural Egyptian cotton 24/3 @ 6000 yds. per lb.

WEFT: Same as warp

WARP ENDS: 800

ENDS PER INCH: 18

REED: 9

WIDTH IN REED: 44″ + 4 dents

DENTING: 2 per dent

THREAD:
2, 1, 2, 1 once
2, 6, 2, 1, 5, 1, 2, 4, 2, 1, 3, 1 ×66
2, 1, 2, 1 once

TREADLING: 1, 3, 1, 2, 4, 2, 1, 5, 1, 2, 6, 2

REQUIREMENTS: For 1 yd.
Warp and weft, 5 oz.

WARP: Peacock 4 ply cotton @ 2700 yds. per lb.

WEFT: Same as warp

WARP ENDS: 675

ENDS PER INCH: 15

REED: 15

WIDTH IN REED: 45″

DENTING: 1 per dent

THREAD: One to heddle
3, 4, 3, 4, 3,
2, 1, 2, 1, 2

TREADLING:
1, 2, 1, 2, 1
3, 4, 3, 4, 3

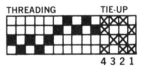

THREADING   TIE-UP

4 3 2 1

TABLE LOOMS:
For pedal 1 use levers 1 + 3
For pedal 2 use levers 1 + 2 + 4
For pedal 3 use levers 2 + 4
For pedal 4 use levers 1 + 3 + 4

REQUIREMENTS: For 1 yd.
Warp and weft, 1395 yds.
Upholstery fabric may be woven on this warp. See page 34.

DOUBLE WIDTH CASEMENT CLOTH

4 harness, 4 pedal

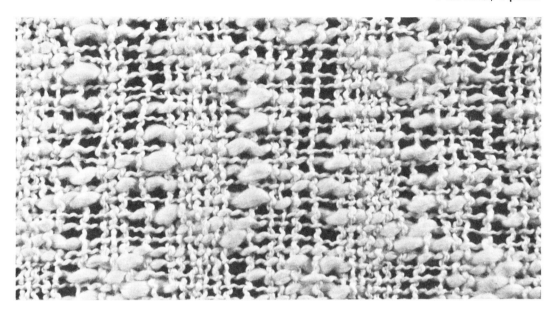

4 3 2 1

WARP: Natural cotton ratine @ 1450 yds. per lb.

WEFT: Natural cotton flake @ 1250 yds. per lb.

WARP ENDS: 296

ENDS PER INCH: 12 on loom
6 off loom

REED: 15

WIDTH IN REED: 24″ + 7 dents
Curtain, 49″

THREAD: Single in heddle 1, 2, 3, 4

TREADLING: To begin, throw shuttle from the right. 1, 2, 3, 4

TABLE LOOMS:
For pedal 1 use levers 1 + 2 + 3
For pedal 2 use levers 1 + 3 + 4
For pedal 3 use lever 1
For pedal 4 use lever 3

REQUIREMENTS: For 1 yd.
Warp, 296 yds.
Weft, 490 yds.

DENTING: Important: After ends have been threaded through the heddles, remove the first end on harness one and discard, then proceed with spaced denting—FROM RIGHT

ONCE
{
1 per dent
1 empty dent
2 per dent
2 empty dents
2 per dent for 2 dents
}

×12
{
4 empty dents
2 per dent
4 empty dents
2 per dent for 3 dents
4 empty dents
2 per dent
4 empty dents
2 per dent for 2 dents
1 empty dent
2 per dent for 3 dents
1 empty dent
2 per dent for 2 dents
}

Below are possible widths on standard size looms.

20" loom
Possible width: 37"
Width in reed: 18" + 7 dents
Ends: 224

36" loom
Possible width: 69"
Width in reed: 34" + 7 dents
Ends: 416

45" loom
Possible width: 89"
Width in reed: 44" + 7 dents
Ends: 536

Actually a very simple weave but great care must be taken to tread correctly otherwise the two layers will be woven together. Check often to see two selvages at the left. The center of the fabric will be on the right.

CURTAIN-BEDSPREAD FABRIC 4 harness, 4 pedal

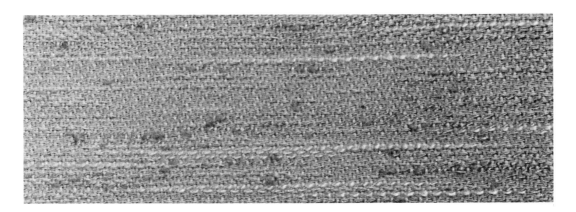

THREADING TIE-UP

4 3 2 1

BROKEN TWILL

WARP: Unmercerized 20/2 natural cotton @ 8400 yds. per lb.

WEFT: Chartreuse rayon flake @ 4500 yds. per lb. / White slub rayon @ 3500 yds. per lb. } Wound together

WARP ENDS: 1080
ENDS PER INCH: 24
REED: 12
WIDTH IN REED: 45"
DENTING: 2 per dent
THREAD: Single in heddle 1, 2, 3, 4

TREADLING: 1, 2, 3, 4
TABLE LOOM:
For pedal 1 use lever 4
For pedal 2 use lever 3
For pedal 3 use lever 1
For pedal 4 use lever 2
REQUIREMENTS: For 1 yd.
Warp, 1080 yds.
Chartreuse flake, 1170 yds.
White slub, 1170 yds.

SHEER CASEMENT DRAPERY

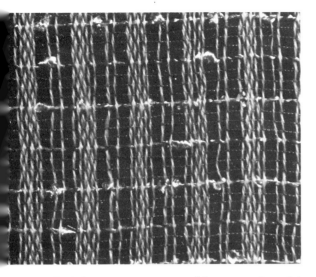

PLAIN WEAVE   4 harness, 2 pedal

WARP: White 15/2 nylon-orlon @ 4200 yds. per lb.

WEFT:
White 20/1 linen—gold twist @ 5000 yds.
White rayon bouclé knot @ 1250 yds.
White rayon bouclé @ 1700 yds. per lb.

WARP ENDS: 540

ENDS PER INCH: 12

REED: 15

WIDTH IN REED: 45″

DENTING:
2 per dent for 3 dents
3 empty dents
2 per one dent
3 empty dents

THREAD: Single in heddle 1, 2, 3, 4

TREADLING:
Linen 1, 2, 1
Bouclé 2
Linen 1, 2, 1
Knot 2
Repeat

TABLE LOOMS:
For pedal 1 use levers 1 + 3
For pedal 2 use levers 2 + 4

REQUIREMENTS: For 1 yd.
Warp, 542 yds.
Knot, 45 yds.
Bouclé, 45 yds.
Linen, 270 yds.
May be woven on the same warp as on page 40.

4 harness, 4 pedal

OVERSHOT

WARP: Soft twist 10/3 cotton @ 2800 yds. per lb. Coral pink or any light color.

WEFT: White spun viscose @ 1200 yds. per lb.

WARP ENDS: 648

ENDS PER INCH: 18

REED: 9

WIDTH IN REED: 36″

DENTING: 2 per dent

THREAD: Single in heddle
4, 3, 4, 3, 2, 3, 4, 3, 4
1, 2, 1, 2, 3, 2, 1, 2, 1

TREADLING: 1, 2, 1, 4, 3, 2, 3, 4

TABLE LOOMS:
For pedal 1 use levers 1 + 2
For pedal 2 use levers 1 + 4
For pedal 3 use levers 3 + 4
For pedal 4 use levers 2 + 3

REQUIREMENTS: For 1 yd.
Warp, 648 yds.
Weft, 1008 yds.
May be woven on the same warp as on page 41.

SHEER CASEMENT

4 harness, 2 pedal

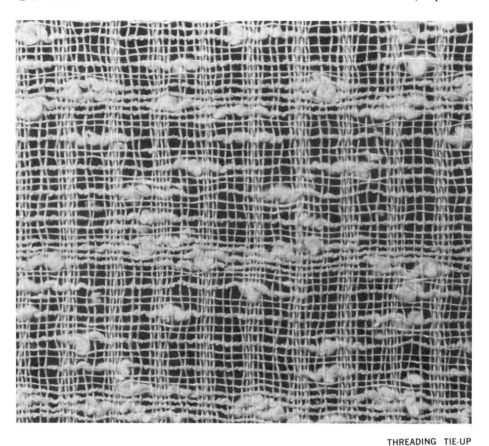

THREADING TIE-UP

2 1

PLAIN WEAVE

WARP: White 15/2 nylon-orlon @ 4200 yds. per lb.
WEFT: Natural cotton flake @ 1700 yds. White rayon slub @ 3500 yds.
WARP ENDS: 540
ENDS PER INCH: 12
REED: 15
WIDTH IN REED: 45″
DENTING:
2 per dent for 3 dents
3 empty dents
2 per one dent
3 empty dents
THREAD: Single in heddle 1, 2, 3, 4

TREADLING:
4 flake 1, 2, 1, 2 beat together
2 rayon 1, 2 ⎫
1 flake 1 ⎪
2 rayon 2, 1 ⎬ ×2
1 flake 2 ⎭
2 rayon 1, 2
Repeat

TABLE LOOMS:
For pedal 1 use levers 1 + 3
For pedal 2 use levers 2 + 4

REQUIREMENTS: For 1 yd.
Warp, 542 yds.
Flake, 450 yds.
Slub, 630 yds.
May be woven on the same warp as on page 39.

CURTAIN 4 harness, 2 pedal

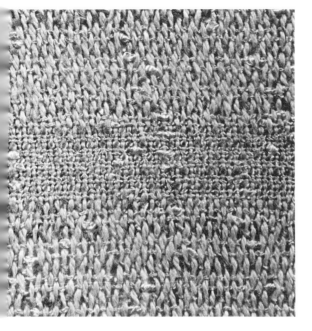

DRAPERY 4 harness, 3 pedal

THREADING   **TIE-UP**

3 2 1

PLAIN WEAVE

WARP: Natural 10/2 ramie @ 1500 yds.
WEFT: Jute and rayon twist @ 1200 yds.
per lb.
Natural rayon nub @ 1300 yds.
per lb.
WARP ENDS: 540
ENDS PER INCH: 12
REED: 12
WIDTH IN REED: 45″
DENTING: 1 per dent
THREAD: 1, 2, 3, 4

THREADING   TIE-UP

2 1

TREADLING:
Jute and rayon 1
Nub 2, 1
Jute and rayon 2
Nub 1, 2
24 shots, very light beat
18 shots, firm beat

TABLE LOOMS:
For pedal 1 use levers 1 + 3
For pedal 2 use levers 2 + 4

REQUIREMENTS: For 1 yd.
Warp, 540 yds.
Jute & rayon, 210 yds.
Rayon nub, 420 yds.

WARP: Soft twist 10/3 cotton @ 2800 yds.
Coral pink or any light color.
WEFT: White spun viscose @ 1200 yds.
per lb.
WARP ENDS: 648
ENDS PER INCH: 18
REED: 9
WIDTH IN REED: 36″
DENTING: 2 per dent
THREAD: Single in heddle
4, 3, 4, 3, 2, 3, 4, 3, 4
1, 2, 1, 2, 3, 2, 1, 2, 1

TREADLING: 1, 2, 3, 2
TABLE LOOMS:
Levers: 2 + 4
3
1 + 4
3

REQUIREMENTS: For 1 yd.
Warp, 648 yds.
Weft, 756 yds.
May be woven on the same warp as on
page 39.

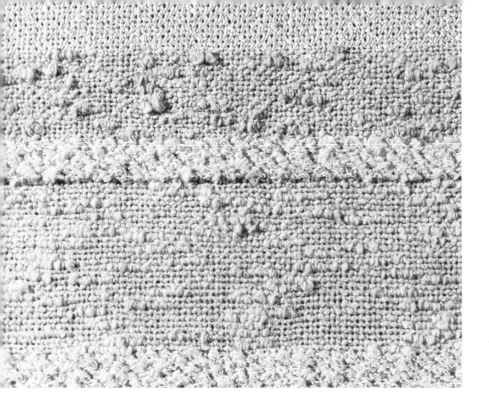

DRAPERY

4 harness, 6 pedal

THREADING TIE-UP

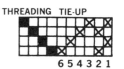

6 5 4 3 2 1

WARP: Ecru mercerized 5/2 cotton @ 2100 yds. per lb.

WEFT:

Fine natural rayon bouclé @ 2200 yds. per lb.

Heavy natural rayon-cotton bouclé @ 650 yds. per lb.

Natural cotton nub @ 900 yds. per lb.

Dk. ecru cotton nub @ 900 yds. per lb.

WARP ENDS: 672

ENDS PER INCH: 15

REED: 15

WIDTH IN REED: 45" less 3 dents

DENTING: 1 per dent

THREAD: Single in heddle 1, 2, 3, 4

REQUIREMENTS: For 1 yd.

Warp, 672 yds.

Fine bouclé, 600 yds.

Heavy bouclé, 61 yds.

Natural nub, 118 yds.

Dk. ecru nub, 123 yds.

TREADLING:

8 inches fine bouclé 1, 2

1 inch dk. ecru nub 1,2

8 shots heavy bouclé 3, 4, 5, 6 ×2

1¾ inch natural nub, 1, 2

8 shots heavy bouclé 3, 4, 5, 6 ×2

1 inch dk. ecru nub 1, 2

Repeat

TABLE LOOMS:

For pedal 1 use levers 2 + 4

For pedal 2 use levers 1 + 3

For pedal 3 use lever 4

For pedal 4 use lever 3

For pedal 5 use lever 2

For pedal 6 use lever 1

DRAPERY

PLAIN WEAVE

WARP: 20/2 rayon @ 8400 yds. per lb.
    Cherry
    Deep violet
    Fuchsia
    Lt. green
    Dk. green
    Royal
    Black

WEFT: Emerald rayon bouclé ⎫
    Dk. green 2 ply wool ⎬ Wound together
    spun nylon ⎭

WARP ENDS: 1208

ENDS PER INCH: 27

REED: 12

WIDTH IN REED: 44″ + 5 dents

DENTING:
4 per dent for 5 dents ⎫ ×44
1 per dent for 7 dents ⎭
4 per dent for 5 dents

THREAD: Single in heddle 1, 2, 3, 4 but not necessarily in warping order. Thread any end that comes up.

TREADLING: 1, 2

TABLE LOOMS:
Levers: 1 + 3
       2 + 4

WARPING ORDER: Warp several ends together
2 cherry
2 violet
2 fuchsia
2 violet
2 fuchsia
2 cherry
2 royal
2 lt. green
2 dk. green
2 royal
2 fuchsia
2 cherry
2 violet
1 black
———
27 ends = 1″

THREADING   TIE-UP

    2 1

REQUIREMENTS: For 1 yd.
WARP:
Cherry, 270 yds.
Violet, 270 yds.
Fuchsia, 270 yds.
Lt. green, 90 yds.
Dk. green, 90 yds.
Royal, 180 yds.
Black, 45 yds.
WEFT:
Bouclé, 630 yds.
Nylon, 630 yds.

CURTAIN

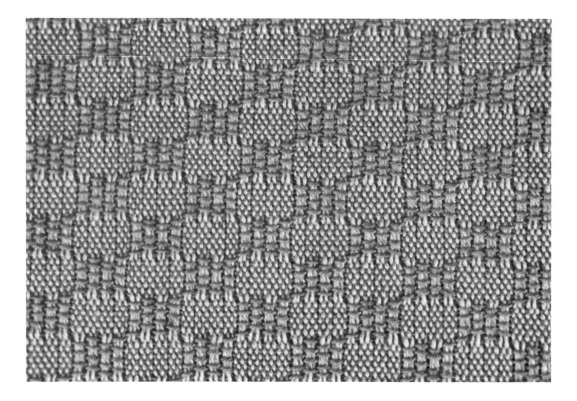

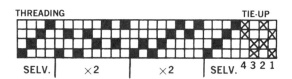

M'S AND O'S

WARP: Natural 8/2 soft twist cotton @
3360 yds. per lb.

WEFT: Yellow 8/2 cotton same as warp

WARP ENDS: 1056 + 8 selv. = 1064

ENDS PER INCH: 24

REED: 12

WIDTH IN REED: 44″ + selvages

DENTING: 2 per dent

THREAD: Single in heddle
Selv. 4, 3, 2, 1
4, 3, 4, 3, 2, 1, 2, 1 ×2
4, 2, 4, 2, 3, 1, 3, 1 ×2
Selv. 4, 3, 2, 1

TREADLING:
1, 2 ×4
3, 4 ×4

TABLE LOOMS:
Levers: $\left.\begin{array}{l} 1+3 \\ 2+4 \end{array}\right\}$ ×4
$\left.\begin{array}{l} 1+2 \\ 3+4 \end{array}\right\}$ ×4

REQUIREMENTS: For 1 yd.
Warp, 1064 yds.
Weft, 1064 yds.

DRAPERY 4 harness, 2 pedal

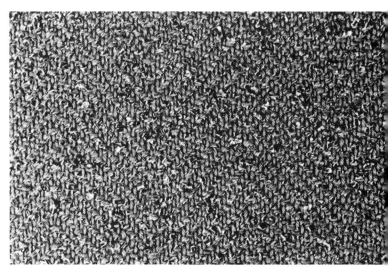

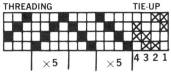

HERRINGBONE

PLAIN WEAVE

WARP: 8/2 Swedish 1/2 bleached linen @ approx. 1200 yds. per lb.

WEFT: Natural soft spun rayon ratine @ 800 yds. per lb.

WARP ENDS: 480

REED: 15

WIDTH IN REED: 44"

DENTING:
1 per dent for 48 dents ⎫
20 empty dents   ⎬ ×9
1 per dent for 48 dents ⎭

THREAD: Single in heddle 1, 2, 3, 4

TREADLING: 1, 2

TABLE LOOMS:
Levers: 1 + 3
        2 + 4

REQUIREMENTS: For 1 yd.
Warp, 480 yds.
Weft, 660 yds.

WARP: Medium green soft twist 10/3 cotton @ 2800 yds. per lb.

WEFT: Lt. green rayon bouclé @ 1700 yds. per lb. ⎫
Med. 10/3 cotton same as warp ⎬ Wound together ⎭

WARP ENDS: 874

ENDS PER INCH: 20

REED: 10

WIDTH IN REED: 43" + 7 dents

DENTING: 2 per dent

THREAD: Single in heddle
1, 2, 3, 4 ×5
1, 2, 3
4, 3, 2, 1 ×5
4, 3, 2
Repeat ×19

TREADLING: 1, 2, 3, 4

TABLE LOOMS:
Levers: 3 + 4
        1 + 4
        1 + 2
        2 + 3

REQUIREMENTS: For 1 yd.
10/3 cotton warp and weft, 1666 yds.
Bouclé, 792 yds.

DRAPERY

4 harness, 6 pedal

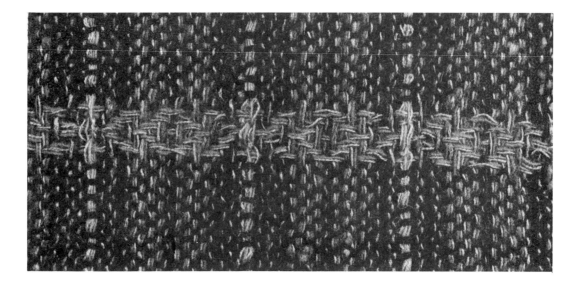

THREADING   **TIE-UP**

1 DENT   6 5 4 3 2 1

WARP:

7/1 wool @ 3900 yds. per lb.
   Red
   Green
   Black
7/2 douppioni silk @ 5800 yds. per lb.
   Scarlet
   Emerald
   Royal Blue
   Purple

WEFT:

7/1 red wool } Wound
7/2 scarlet silk} together
10/2 black wool} Wound
7/2 black silk } together

WARP ENDS: 874

ENDS PER INCH: 20

REED: 9

WIDTH IN REED: 43″ + 7 dents

DENTING:

2 per dent for 17 dents
6 per dent once

THREAD: 2 per heddle (1 wool + 1 silk)
Follow warping order
1, 2, 3, 4 ×2
1
4, 3, 2, 1 ×2
4, 3, 4

WARPING ORDER:

A [1 black wool / 1 blue silk] ×4
B [1 green wool / 1 emerald silk] ×4
C [1 black wool / 1 purple silk]
Repeat B
Repeat A
D [1 red wool / 1 scarlet silk] ×3
Repeat the whole 21 times
Repeat to D

TREADLING:

3″ black 1, 2
7 red 3, 4, 5, 6, 5, 4, 3

TABLE LOOMS:

For pedal 1 use levers 1 + 3
For pedal 2 use levers 2 + 4
For pedal 3 use levers 1 + 4
For pedal 4 use levers 3 + 4
For pedal 5 use levers 2 + 3
For pedal 6 use levers 1 + 2

REQUIREMENTS: For 1 yd.

4 oz. wool
3 oz. silk

(46)

PILLOWS

The knife-edge pillow is the most satisfactory type for hand woven pillow covers. To make, simply fold one side, seam two sides, insert stuffing or pillow form, and whip stitch the fourth side. Welting or fringe in the seam is optional, and for the most part, unnecessary. It may even detract from the general effectiveness of some covers.

To give pillows a custom-made look, weave the pattern on the front side only. Continue weaving the back in solid color, usually the ground color used for the pattern side.

Pillows may be woven singly or in pairs.

If only a few pillow covers are to be woven, probably single width is the better, in which case the warp is set the width of the pillow plus shrinkage, which is 2″ to 3″ depending on the type of yarns used.

To weave a pair of pillows at the same time, set the warp twice the width of one pillow plus shrinkage and seam allowance. Add one contrasting warp end in the center of the warp, heddle and dent it along with a center warp end. Use this later as a cutting guide to separate the two pillows. Machine stitch on either side of the guide line before cutting. The two front sides will be woven at the same time, as will the backs.

Many completely different pillows may be woven on the same warp by simply weaving with yarns of different colors, sizes, and textures.

At the bottom of many patterns, other patterns which may be woven on the same warp are listed. Only the tie-up and treadling need be changed.

By using the same color warp set @ 240 or 270 ends, pillows on pages 52, 54, 55, 56, 57, 58, 60 and 61 may all be woven on the same warp.

Standard sizes for knife-edge pillows are 14″, 16″, 18″, and 20″ square, 10″ × 20″, 13″ × 20″, and 18″ × 27″. Of these, 16″ square is the size mostly preferred. A warp set at 18″ will weave approximately 16″ plus enough to turn in for seaming.

For lightweight covers, seaming is done in the usual way, either by hand, or machine stitched, pressed open and turned.

For covers woven of many bulky yarns it is best to work right side out, turn in the selvages, and blind or whip stitch, using warp yarn as a sewing thread.

Standard size pillow forms are available, but a percale or muslin inner cover made for each pillow gives the nicest fit. The inner cover should be seamed ½″ larger than the finished woven cover. This gives the fabric a chance to stretch over the form.

Down or dacron is excellent for stuffing. Dacron gives a lightweight pillow, is easy to work with, and available in 8 oz. packages, enough for an 18″ cut-size pillow. A little extra stuffed well up in each corner of the muslin cover makes for a better looking pillow.

Almost any yarns on hand will weave up into colorful pillows. Use yarns singly or several together to build up size of weft. Pillows are a wonderful way to use up all those lovely bits of left-over yarns. Fingering yarn makes a good pillow warp in place of soft cotton. Knitting yarn is an excellent pillow weft. Both yarns are easily obtainable, come in many colors in small quantities and most of them are washable.

Some of the pillow patterns may be enlarged upon to weave fabrics for other uses, such as spreads, draperies, bags, purses and even skirts.

PILLOW

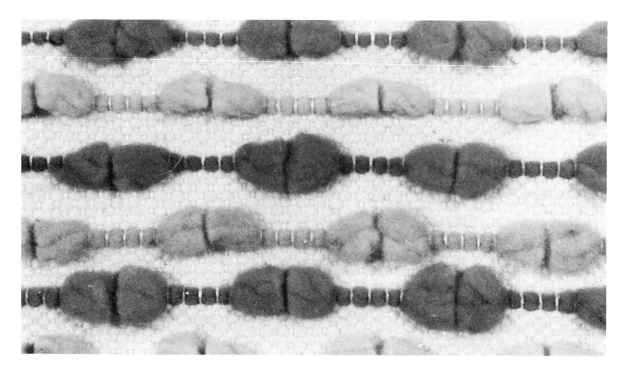

THREADING   TIE-UP

4 3 2 1

WARP: Natural mercerized pearl cotton 5

WEFT: Natural eiderdown @ 480 yds. per
4 oz. skein
     Mexican handspun or rug yarn
        Yellow
        Orange

WARP ENDS: 190

ENDS PER INCH: 10

REED: 10

WIDTH IN REED: 19″

DENTING: 1 per dent

THREAD:
4, 3 ×5 ⎫
2, 1 ×5 ⎬ ×9
4, 3 ×5 ⎭

TREADLING: 4″ natural 1, 2
Skip 20 warp threads
Tread 3 ⎫
Center yellow, leave ¾″ tails ⎪
10 natural 1, 2 ×5 ⎬ ×8
Skip 30 warp threads ⎪
Tread 4 ⎪
Center orange, leave ¾″ tails ⎭
Repeat yellow
22″ natural 1, 2
Cut through floats

TABLE LOOMS:
For pedal 1 use levers 2 + 4
For pedal 2 use levers 1 + 3
For pedal 3 use lever 4
For pedal 4 use lever 1

(48)

PILLOW

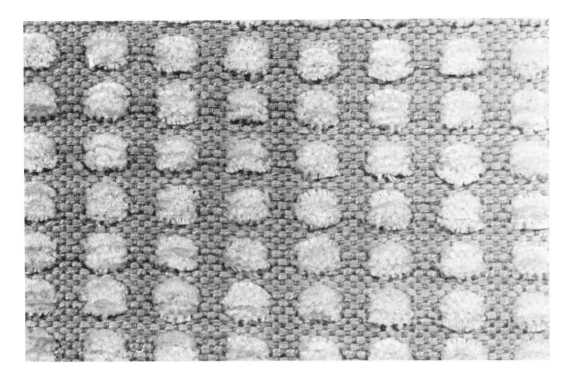

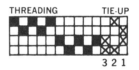

THREADING   TIE-UP

3 2 1

WARP: Unmercerized light grey cotton
16/2 or 20/2

WEFT:

Ground

2 lt. yellow rayon flake
2 lt. yellow 7/1 wool   } Wound on
1 med. yellow 8/1   one bobbin
    cotton

Pattern

3 natural 12 cut rayon chenille on
one bobbin

WARP ENDS: 432

ENDS PER INCH: 24 @ 2 per heddle

REED: 12

WIDTH IN REED: 18″

DENTING: 2 per dent

THREAD: Doubled in heddle

2, 1, 2, 1, 2 } × 21
4, 3, 4, 3, 4
2, 1, 2, 1, 2, 1

TREADLING: Front

Yellow 1, 2, 1, 2, 1, 2
Natural 3
Yellow 1
Natural 3
Yellow 2
Natural 3
Repeat for 18″

Back

Yellow 1, 2 for 18″

TABLE LOOMS:

For pedal 1 use levers 2 + 3
For pedal 2 use levers 1 + 4
For pedal 3 use levers 1 + 2
May be woven on the same warp as on
    pages 50, 51, 53, 55, 59.

PILLOW

4 harness, 3 pedal

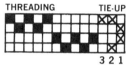

3 2 1

WARP: Unmercerized light grey cotton 16/2 or 20/2

WEFT:

Ground

1 gold-white rayon bouclé
1 pale grey rayon flake
1 lt. grey 7/1 wool
} Wound on one bobbin

Pattern

2½" cut lengths of rug wool
Apple green
Soft rose pink

WARP ENDS: 432

ENDS PER INCH: 24 @ 2 per heddle

REED: 12

WIDTH IN REED: 18"

DENTING: 2 per dent

THREAD: Doubled in heddle

2, 1, 2, 1, 2
4, 3, 4, 3, 4
} ×21

2, 1, 2, 1, 2, 1

May be woven on the same warp as on pages 49, 51, 53, 55, 59.

TREADLING: 3" ground 1, 2

1 ground shot between every pattern shot

A—Tread 3

Center one green under the middle 3 groups of warp threads.

Skip 3 groups of warp threads to the right and center one green.

Skip 3 groups to the left and center third green.

Use firm beat.

Repeat using rose wool.

Repeat using green wool.

B—Tread 3

Center one green under 3 groups of warp threads in each of the two spaces between the first band.

Repeat using rose

Repeat using green

Weave A, B × 12 + A

Weave 20" ground on 1, 2

TABLE LOOMS:

For pedal 1 use levers 2 + 3

For pedal 2 use levers 1 + 4

For pedal 3 use lever 4

PILLOW 4 harness, 3 pedal

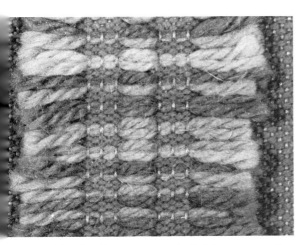

WARP: Unmercerized light grey cotton 16/2 or 20/2

WEFT:
4 ply bright rose knitting wool
Rug wool: 2½″ cut lengths
    Lt. yellow
    Yellow
    Gold color

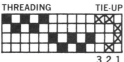

WARP ENDS: 432

ENDS PER INCH: 24 @ 2 per heddle

REED: 12

WIDTH IN REED: 18″

DENTING: 2 per dent

THREAD: Doubled in heddle
$\left. \begin{array}{l} 2, 1, 2, 1, 2 \\ 4, 3, 4, 3, 4 \end{array} \right\} \times 21$
2, 1, 2, 1, 2, 1

TREADLING: 1″ Rose 1, 2
For inlay:
2 lengths wool per inlay
Random colors
Tread 3
Count off 9 groups of warp threads in the
    middle, center wool under next 2 groups
    to the left and to the right.
Weave rose 1, 2, 1, 2
Repeat for 17″
Back: Weave 18″ rose 1, 2
Beat firmly

TABLE LOOMS:
For pedal 1 use levers 2 + 3
For pedal 2 use levers 1 + 4
For pedal 3 use lever 4
May be woven on the same warp as on
    pages 49, 50, 53, 55, 59.

PILLOW 4 harness, 6 pedal

HONEYCOMB

WARP: Mercerized natural pearl cotton 5
WEFT: Lt. yellow swedish cowhair
    Natural heavy rug yarn

WARP ENDS: 200

ENDS PER INCH: 10

REED: 10

WIDTH IN REED: 20″

DENTING: 1 per dent

THREAD:
4, 3 ×5
2, 1 ×5

TREADLING:
1″ yellow 1, 2
$\left. \begin{array}{l} \text{Natural 1} \\ 6 \text{ yellow 3, 4} \times 3 \\ \text{Natural 2} \\ 6 \text{ yellow 5, 6} \times 3 \end{array} \right\}$ Repeat for 16″
Natural 1
17″ yellow 2, 1

TABLE LOOMS:
For pedal 1 use levers 1 + 3
For pedal 2 use levers 2 + 4
For pedal 3 use levers 1 + 2 + 3
For pedal 4 use levers 1 + 2 + 4
For pedal 5 use levers 1 + 3 + 4
For pedal 6 use levers 2 + 3 + 4
May be woven on the same warp as on
    page 57.

RYA PILLOW

PILLOW

WARP: Unmercerized natural 10/2 cotton

WEFT:

1 lt. yellow 7/1 wool ⎫
1 med. yellow 7/1 wool ⎬ Wound together
1 lemon rayon flake ⎭

Knots—10 threads mercerized natural pearl cotton 5

WARP ENDS: 270

ENDS PER INCH: 15

REED: 15

WIDTH IN REED: 18″

DENTING: 1 per dent

THREAD: 1, 2, 3, 4, end on H.2

TREADLING: 1, 2, 3, 4

6″ yellow

1 row knots ⎫
2″ yellow ⎬ ×3

1 row knots

23″ yellow

Knots are made over 2 pair (4) warp ends. Skip 2 warp ends between knots.

For rya knots: see page 104

TABLE LOOMS:

For pedal 1 use levers 3 + 4
For pedal 2 use levers 2 + 3
For pedal 3 use levers 1 + 2
For pedal 4 use levers 1 + 4

THREADING TIE-UP

4 3 2 1

WARP: Unmercerized orange 8/2 cotton

WEFT: 3 ply shiny cotton @ 400 yds. per lb.

Yellow
Orange

WARP ENDS: 240

ENDS PER INCH: 15

REED: 15

WIDTH IN REED: 16″

DENTING: 1 per dent

THREAD: 1, 2, 3, 4

TREADLING:

10 yellow 1, 2 ⎫
10 orange 1, 2 ⎬ ×7

20 yellow 1, 2 **center**

10 orange 1, 2 ⎫
10 yellow 1, 2 ⎬ ×7

TABLE LOOMS:

For pedal 1 use levers 1 + 2
For pedal 2 use levers 3 + 4

May be woven on the same warp as on pages 54 and 55

THREADING TIE-UP

2 1

PILLOW

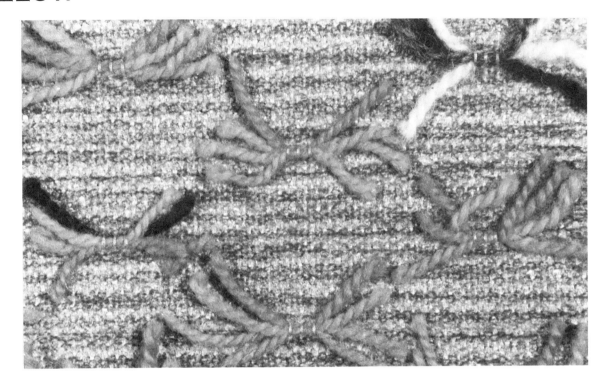

THREADING   TIE-UP

4 3 2 1

WARP: Unmercerized light grey cotton 16/2 or 20/2

WEFT:

Ground

    12 cut variegated grey rayon chenille

Pattern

    Rya wool cut to 2½″ lengths
      Orange
      Pink
      Cerise
      A few lt., med., dk. grey and natural white

WARP ENDS: 432

ENDS PER INCH: 24 @ 2 per heddle

REED: 12

WIDTH IN REED: 18″

DENTING: 2 per dent

THREAD: Doubled in heddle

2, 1, 2, 1, 2 ⎫
           ⎬ ×21
4, 3, 4, 3, 4 ⎭

2, 1, 2, 1, 2, 1

TREADLING: 3″ grey 1, 2

Pattern—Tread 3

A—Inlay 4 wool lengths under center group of 3 warp threads.

Skip 4 groups to the left and 4 to the right and inlay wool lengths.

Beat firmly

Weave 1¼″ grey 1, 2

B—Tread 4

Center wool pieces in each of the two spaces between first three inlays.

Weave 1¼″ grey 1, 2

Weave A + B × 5 + A

Weave 20″ grey 1, 2

TABLE LOOMS:

For pedal 1 use levers 2 + 3

For pedal 2 use levers 1 + 4

For pedal 3 use lever 4

For pedal 4 use lever 2

May be woven on the same warp as on pages 49, 50, 51, 55, 59.

CHAIR BACK PILLOW 8" x 16"

4 harness, 6 pedal

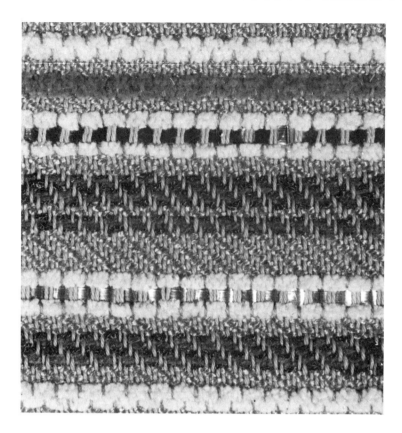

TREADLING:

3" orange 1, 2, 3, 4 ×12
*2 yellow chenille 5, 6
4 orange 1, 2, 3, 4
4 purple 1, 2, 3, 4
4 orange 1, 2, 3, 4
1 yellow chenille 5
1 gold fold 3
1 yellow chenille 5
8 orange 3, 4, 1, 2 ×2
2 purple 3, 4
2 orange 1, 2
4 purple 3, 4, 1, 2
4 orange 3, 4, 1, 2
1 yellow chenille 6
1 red fold 2
1 yellow chenille 6
4 orange 1, 2, 3, 4
2 red chenille 5, 6
4 orange 1, 2, 3, 4
2 yellow chenille 5, 6
4 orange 1, 2, 3, 4
*2 red chenille 5, 6
4 orange 1, 2, 3, 4
2 purple 1, 2
2 orange 3, 4
1 yellow chenille 5
1 gold fold 3
1 yellow chenille 5
4 orange 3, 4, 1, 2
2 purple 3, 4
4 orange 1, 2, 3, 4
1 yellow chenille 5
1 red fold 3 **center**
Repeat in reverse, 1 yellow, etc.

TABLE LOOMS:
For pedal 1 use levers 3 + 4
For pedal 2 use levers 2 + 3
For pedal 3 use levers 1 + 2
For pedal 4 use levers 1 + 4
For pedal 5 use lever 3
For pedal 6 use lever 1
To make: seam two selvages together; seam one end; insert pillow and whip other end.
* Shown in photo

THREADING   TIE-UP

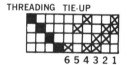

6 5 4 3 2 1

WARP: Unmercerized orange 8/2 cotton
WEFT: Orange 2 ply spun viscose
       8 cut lt. yellow chenille—doubled
       8 cut red chenille—doubled
       3/16" metallic flatfold
         Red
         Green gold
       Fuchsia wool spun rayon⎫ Wound
       Purple rayon bouclé   ⎭ together
WARP ENDS: 270
ENDS PER INCH: 15
REED: 15
WIDTH IN REED: 18"
DENTING: 1 per dent
THREAD: 1, 2, 3, 4, end on H.2

PILLOWS

4 harness, 6 pedal

4 harness, 4 pedal

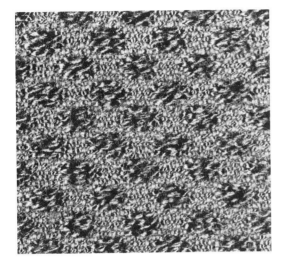

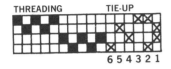

THREADING   TIE-UP

6 5 4 3 2 1

WARP: Unmercerized light grey cotton 16/2 or 20/2

WEFT: Rust 2 ply spun viscose @ 840 yds.

WARP ENDS: 432

ENDS PER INCH: 24 @ 2 per heddle

REED: 12

WIDTH IN REED: 18″

DENTING: 2 per dent

THREAD: Doubled in heddle

2, 1, 2, 1, 2
4, 3, 4, 3, 4 } ×21
2, 1, 2, 1, 2, 1

TREADLING:

1, 2
3, 1, 5, 2, 5, 1, 3
2, 1
4, 2, 6, 1, 6, 2, 4

TABLE LOOMS:

For pedal 1 use levers 2 + 3
For pedal 2 use levers 1 + 4
For pedal 3 use lever 4
For pedal 4 use lever 2
For pedal 5 use lever 3
For pedal 6 use lever 1

May be woven on the same warp as on pages 49, 50, 51, 53, 59.

WARP: Unmercerized orange 8/2 cotton

WEFT: Orange 2 ply spun viscose

Variegated yellow-white rayon bouclé } Wound together
Fine 2 ply yellow dacron

Fuchsia wool spun rayon } Wound together
Purple rayon bouclé

WARP ENDS: 240

ENDS PER INCH: 15

REED: 15

WIDTH IN REED: 16″

DENTING: 1 per dent

THREAD: 1, 2, 3, 4

TREADLING: 4, 3, 2, 1

Orange 2″
10 yellow
 7 orange
 5 purple
 2 yellow } ×6
 2 orange
 2 purple
 4 orange
10 yellow
Orange 16½″

THREADING   TIE-UP

4 3 2 1

TABLE LOOMS:

For pedal 1 use levers 3 + 4
For pedal 2 use levers 2 + 3
For pedal 3 use levers 1 + 2
For pedal 4 use levers 1 + 4

May be woven on the same warp as on pages 52, 54.

PILLOWS

THREADING   TIE-UP

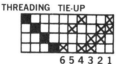

6 5 4 3 2 1

WARP: Unmercerized bright rose 8/2 cotton

WEFT: Rose 2 ply cotton @ 600 yds. per lb. } Wound together
Lt. rose 8/2 rayon
Natural 3 cut chenille
Lt. red 6 cut chenille
Orange 6 cut chenille
3 ply shiny cotton @ 400 yds. per lb.
    Lemon, yellow and orange
3/16" green gold metallic flatfold

WARP ENDS: 270

ENDS PER INCH: 15

REED: 15

WIDTH IN REED: 18"

DENTING: 1 per dent

THREAD: 1, 2, 3, 4, end on H.2

TREADLING:
3½" rose 1, 3
*6 red chenille 1, 3 ×3
 9 rose 1, 3 ×4 + 1
 3 orange chenille 3, 1, 3
 6 orange cotton 2, 1, 4, 3, 2, 1
 3 yellow cotton 4, 3, 2
 1 orange cotton 1
 1 yellow cotton 4
 1 orange cotton 3
 1 yellow cotton 2
 2 orange cotton 3, 4
10 lemon cotton 1, 2, 3, 4 ×2 + 1, 2
 2 natural chenille 6, 5
*1 gold fold 3
 2 natural chenille 5, 6
 4 rose 1, 3 ×2
 2 natural chenille 5, 6
CENTER OF FRONT—1 gold fold 1, RE-PEAT IN REVERSE
BACK—17" rose 1, 3

TABLE LOOMS:
For pedal 1 use levers 3 + 4
For pedal 2 use levers 2 + 3
For pedal 3 use levers 1 + 2
For pedal 4 use levers 1 + 4
For pedal 5 use lever 3
For pedal 6 use lever 1
May be woven on the same warp as on pages 57, 61.

*Shown in photo

(56)

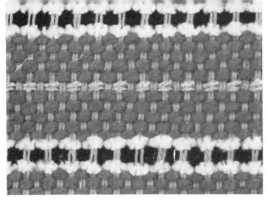

4 harness, 3 pedal

THREADING TIE-UP

3 2 1

Chair pillow 8″ × 22″

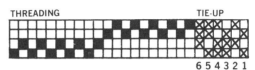

4 harness, 6 pedal

THREADING   TIE-UP

6 5 4 3 2 1

WARP: Unmercerized bright rose 8/2 cotton

WEFT: Rose 2 ply cotton @ ⎫ Wound
     600 yds. per lb. ⎬ together
    Lt. rose 8/2 rayon ⎭
    White 8 cut chenille
    Yellow slub rayon, doubled
    Black stovepipe ribbon folded
      to 3/16″

WARP ENDS: 270

ENDS PER INCH: 15

REED: 15

WIDTH IN REED: 18″

DENTING: 1 per dent

THREAD: 1, 2, 3, 4, end on H.2

TREADLING:

3″ rose 1, 2
1 chenille 3
1 ribbon 2
1 chenille 3
5 rose 2, 1, 2, 1, 2 ⎫
1 yellow 1　　　　　　⎬ ×12
5 rose 2, 1, 2, 1, 2 ⎭
1 chenille 3
1 ribbon 2
1 chenille 3
3″ rose 2, 1

TABLE LOOMS:

For pedal 1 use levers 1 + 2
For pedal 2 use levers 3 + 4
For pedal 3 use lever 1

To make: seam two selvages together; seam one end; insert pillow and whip other end.

May be woven on the same warp as on pages 56, 61.

HONEYCOMB

WARP: Mercerized natural pearl cotton 5

WEFT: Blue 4 ply knitting wool, doubled
     Natural heavy rug yarn

WARP ENDS: 200

ENDS PER INCH: 10

REED: 10

WIDTH IN REED: 20″

DENTING: 1 per dent

THREAD: 4, 3 ×5
     2, 1 ×5

TREADLING:

1″ blue 1, 2
2 natural 1, 2 ⎫
6 blue 3, 4 ×3 ⎪
2 natural 1, 2 ⎬ Repeat for 16″
6 blue 5, 6 ×3 ⎪
2 natural 1, 2 ⎭
17″ blue 1, 2

TABLE LOOMS:

For pedal 1 use levers 1 + 3
For pedal 2 use levers 2 + 4
For pedal 3 use levers 1 + 2 + 3
For pedal 4 use levers 1 + 2 + 4
For pedal 5 use levers 1 + 3 + 4
For pedal 6 use levers 2 + 3 + 4

May be woven on the same warp as on page 51

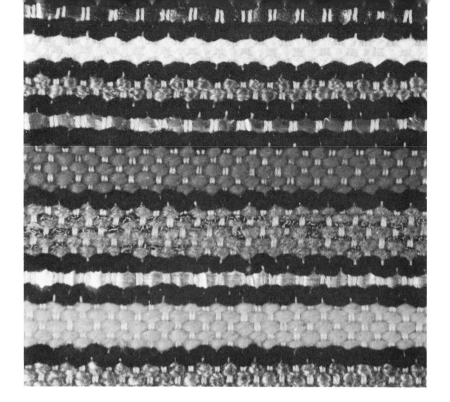

4 harness, 4 pedal

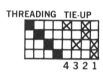
THREADING TIE-UP
4 3 2 1

WARP: Unmercerized cerise 8/2 cotton

WEFT:

2 ply cotton @ 600 yds. per lb.
    Cerise
    Blue

3 ply shiny cotton @ 400 yds. per lb.
    Yellow
    Emerald

³⁄₁₆″ metallic flatfold
    Red
    Blue
    Green gold

Black 6 cut chenille

Fuchsia wool spun rayon ⎫ Wound
Purple rayon bouclé   ⎬ together

WARP ENDS: 240

ENDS PER INCH: 15

REED: 15

WIDTH IN REED: 16″

DENTING: 1 per dent

THREAD: 1, 2, 3, 4

May be woven on the same warp as on page 60.

TREADLING:

2½″ rose 1, 2
  2 black 3, 4
  8 rose 1, 2 ×4
  2 black 3, 4
  1 purple 1
  2 black 4, 3
  2 blue cotton 2, 1
  2 black 4, 3
  1 green 2
  2 black 3, 4
  1 blue fold 1
  2 black 4, 3
  5 yellow 2, 1, 2, 1, 2
  2 black 3, 4
  1 red fold 1
  2 black 4, 3
*5 green 2, 1, 2, 1, 2
  2 black 3, 4
  5 rose 1, 2, 1, 2, 1
  2 black 4, 3
  1 gold fold 2
  2 black 3, 4
  5 purple 1, 2, 1, 2, 1
  2 black 4, 3
  5 blue cotton 2, 1, 2, 1, 2
  2 black 3, 4
  1 red fold 1
  2 black 4, 3
  2 green 2, 1
  2 black 4, 3
  3 yellow 2, 1, 2
  2 black 3, 4
  1 blue fold 1
  2 black 4, 3
*8 rose 2, 1 ×4
  2 black 4, 3
  4 blue cotton 2, 1 ×2
  2 black 4, 3
  1 gold fold 2
  2 black 3, 4
  4 purple 1, 2 ×2
  2 black 3, 4
  6 green 1, 2 ×3
  2 black 3, 4
17″ rose 1, 2

TABLE LOOMS:

For pedal 1 use levers 1 + 2
For pedal 2 use levers 3 + 4
For pedal 3 use lever 2
For pedal 4 use lever 4

*Shown in photo

PILLOWS

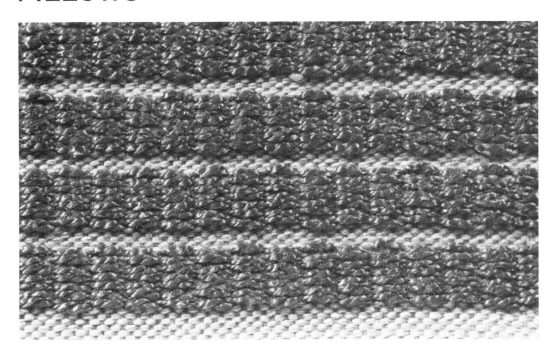

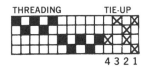

THREADING   TIE-UP

4 3 2 1

WARP: Unmercerized light grey cotton 16/2 or 20/2

WEFT:

Ground

2 fine lt. yellow rayon flake
2 fine 2 ply lemon nylon } Wound on one bobbin
1 gold color 8/1 cotton

Pattern

Orange 2 ply spun viscose

WARP ENDS: 432

ENDS PER INCH: 24 @ 2 per heddle

REED: 12

WIDTH IN REED: 18″

DENTING: 2 per dent

THREAD: Doubled in heddle

2, 1, 2, 1, 2
4, 3, 4, 3, 4 } ×21

2, 1, 2, 1, 2, 1

TREADLING:

3½″ yellow 1, 2

Pattern—Center orange to 12″

A—Orange 3, 4
    Yellow 1
    Orange 4, 3 } ×3
    Yellow 2
    Orange 3, 4
    Yellow 1, 2, 1, 2, 1

B—Orange 4, 3
    Yellow 2
    Orange 3, 4 } ×3
    Yellow 1
    Orange 4, 3
    Yellow 2, 1, 2, 1, 2

Weave A + B × 12 + A

Weave 20″ yellow 1, 2

TABLE LOOMS:

For pedal 1 use levers 1 + 4

For pedal 2 use levers 2 + 3

For pedal 3 use lever 4

For pedal 4 use lever 2

May be woven on the same warp as on pages 49, 50, 51, 53, 55.

(59)

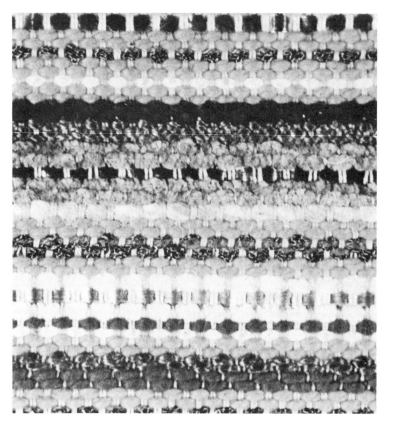

WARP: Unmercerized cerise 8/2 cotton

WEFT:

2 ply cotton @ 600 yds. per lb.
    Brown
    Cerise
    Blue

3 ply shiny cotton @ 400 yds. per lb.
    Emerald
    Lemon

3/16" metallic flatfold
    Red
    Blue
    Green gold

8 cut chenille
    Yellow, doubled
    Olive, doubled
    Royal

Fuchsia wool spun rayon } Wound
Purple rayon bouclé—doubled } together
Viscose and jute twist @ 140 yds. per lb.

WARP ENDS: 240

ENDS PER INCH: 15

REED: 15

WIDTH IN REED: 16"

DENTING: 1 per dent

THREAD: 1, 2, 3, 4

THREADING   TIE-UP

6 5 4 3 2 1

TREADLING: **4 harness, 6 pedal**

2½" brown 1, 2
  1 rose 1
  2 blue chenille 2, 1
  3 emerald 5, 6, 3
  1 rose 2
  1 yellow chenille 1
  1 gold fold 2
  1 yellow chenille 1
  1 rose 2
  1 purple 1
  2 rose 2, 1
  1 red fold 2
  2 rose 1, 2
3" brown 1, 2
*1 purple 1
  2 rose 2, 1
  2 blue 6, 5
  2 emerald 4, 3
  2 rose 2, 1
  1 lemon 2
  1 brown 1
  1 yellow chenille 2
  1 gold fold 1
  1 yellow chenille 2
  2 rose 1, 2
  2 purple 1, 2
  2 rose 1, 2
  1 jute and viscose 1
  2 olive chenille 2, 1
  1 blue fold 2
  2 olive chenille 1, 2
  3 emerald 1, 2, 1
  3 royal chenille 2, 1, 2
  2 rose 1, 2
  1 lemon 1
  2 rose 2, 1
  1 purple 2
  2 rose 1, 2
  1 red fold 1
*2 rose 2, 1
18" brown 2, 1

TABLE LOOMS:

For pedal 1 use levers 3 + 4
For pedal 2 use levers 1 + 2
For pedal 3 use lever 4
For pedal 4 use lever 3
For pedal 5 use lever 2
For pedal 6 use lever 1

May be woven on the same warp as on page 58.

*Shown in photo

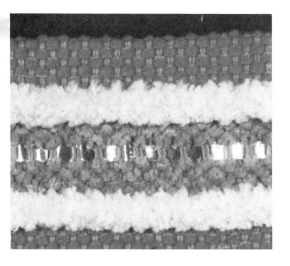
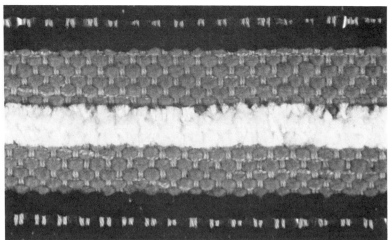

WARP: Unmercerized bright rose 8/2 cotton

WEFT: Rose 2 ply cotton @ 600 yds. per lb. ⎫
Lt. rose 8/2 rayon ⎬ Wound together
Natural 3 cut cotton chenille
Chartreuse 6 cut cotton chenille
Black 8 cut cotton chenille, doubled
3/16" green gold metallic flatfold

WARP ENDS: 270

ENDS PER INCH: 15

REED: 15

WIDTH IN REED: 18"

DENTING: 1 per dent

THREAD: 1, 2, 3, 4

TREADLING:

16 rose, 1, 2 ×8
3 natural 3, 4, 3 ⎫
4 chartreuse 2, 1 ×2 ⎪
1 gold 4 ⎪
4 chartreuse 1, 2 ×2 ⎪
3 natural 3, 4, 3 ⎪
6 rose 2, 1 ×3 ⎬ ×4
3 black 4, 3, 4 ⎪
6 rose 1, 2 ×3 ⎭
3 natural 3, 4, 3
4 chartreuse 2, 1 ×2
1 gold 4
4 chartreuse 1, 2 ×2
3 natural 3, 4, 3
18 inches rose 2, 1

TABLE LOOMS:

For pedal 1 use levers 1 + 2
For pedal 2 use levers 3 + 4
For pedal 3 use lever 2
For pedal 4 use lever 4

WARP: Unmercerized bright rose 8/2 cotton

WEFT: Rose 2 ply cotton @ 600 yds. per lb. ⎫
Lt. rose 8/2 rayon ⎬ Wound together
Natural 3 cut cotton chenille
Black 8 cut cotton chenille, doubled
3/16" red metallic flatfold

WARP ENDS: 270

ENDS PER INCH: 15

REED: 15

WIDTH IN REED: 18"

DENTING: 1 per dent

THREAD: 1, 2, 3, 4, end on H.2

TREADLING:

3 inches rose 1, 2
2 black 3, 4 ⎫
1 red fold 1 ⎪
2 black 4, 3 ⎪
6 rose 2, 1 ×3 ⎬ ×5
2 natural 4, 3 ⎪
6 rose 2, 1 ×3 ⎭
2 black 4, 3
1 red fold 2
2 black 3, 4
20 inches rose 1, 2

THREADING TIE-UP

4 3 2 1

TABLE LOOMS:

For pedal 1 use levers 1 + 2
For pedal 2 use levers 3 + 4
For pedal 3 use lever 2
For pedal 4 use lever 4
Both may be woven on the same warp as on pages 56, 57.

(61)

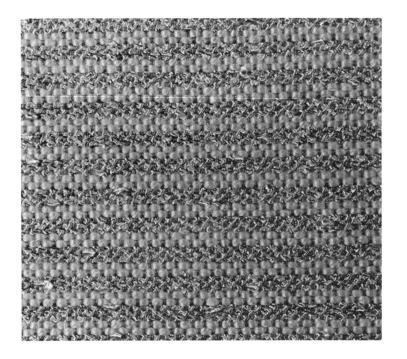

COVERLET 64" x 102"
THROW PILLOWS

4 harness, 2 pedal

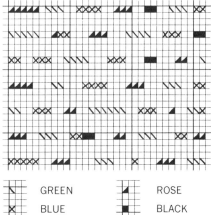

GREEN	ROSE
BLUE	BLACK

RYA KNOTS ON PLAIN WEAVE

THREADING   TIE-UP

2 1

WARP: Unmercerized linen color 20/2 cotton

WEFT: 1 white rayon ratine
1 gold-wrapped white rayon knot } Wound together
White 2 ply soft twist rayon roving
Rya knots on pillows: 3 strands
  Persian rug yarn
    Black
    Green
    Rose
    Shades of blue and
      blue-green

WARP ENDS:
Coverlet 624
Pillow 432

ENDS PER INCH: 24 @ 2 per heddle

REED: 12

WIDTH IN REED:
Coverlet 26"
Pillow 18"

DENTING: 2 per dent

THREAD: Doubled in heddle 1, 2, 3, 4

TREADLING: Coverlet:
  Ratine + knot 1, 2
  Roving 1, 2
Repeat for 10 yds. on loom

Pillow: Remove 4" on either side of warp. Weave 5" same as coverlet ending with roving 1

Rya knots: Count off 44 doubled warp ends at left to begin. Knot in same shed as roving. Each knot over 2 doubled (4) warp ends.
  Fringe: 1" long
Between 7 rows of knots:
  Roving 2
  Ratine + knot 1, 2 } ×3
  Roving 1, 2
  Ratine + knot 1, 2
  Roving 1
Weave 21" same as coverlet
Weave 2nd pillow

TABLE LOOMS:
For pedal 1 use levers 1 + 3
For pedal 2 use levers 2 + 4

REQUIREMENTS: 15 yd. warp for coverlet, 2 pillows and allowances. Amount— 1 lb. 2 oz. 20/2 cotton.

Coverlet is made in three pieces seamed with rope welting.

For rya knots see page 86.

PILLOW

THREADING TIE-UP

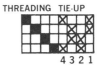

4 3 2 1

WARP: Mercerized pearl cotton 3
   Chocolate
   Olive
   Lt. olive
   Taupe
   Natural
  Eggshell 4/4 soft twist
  Cream 10/3 soft twist

WEFT: Sand crimpset nylon-wool
   Natural rayon knot

WARP ENDS: 160

ENDS PER INCH: 10

REED: 10

WIDTH IN REED: 16″

DENTING: 1 per dent

THREAD: 1, 2, 3, 4 in same order as warp-ing order. Substitute 2 pearl ends for last 2 eggshell on left selvage side.

TREADLING: 1, 2, 3, 4
1 wool
1 rayon knot
Repeat for 32″

WARPING ORDER:
1 chocolate
1 olive
1 eggshell ⎱ ×2
1 natural ⎰
1 olive
1 cream
1 chocolate
1 natural
1 eggshell
1 lt. olive
1 eggshell
1 taupe
1 natural
1 cream
1 lt. olive
1 chocolate
2 eggshell

TABLE LOOMS:
For pedal 1 use levers 3 + 4
For pedal 2 use levers 1 + 2
For pedal 3 use levers 2 + 3
For pedal 4 use levers 1 + 4

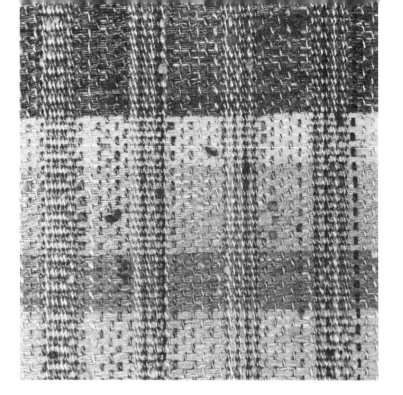

PILLOW

4 harness, 2 pedal

THREADING TIE-UP

2 1

PLAIN WEAVE

WARP: 20/2 mercerized pearl cotton
        Skipper blue
        Violet
        Heliotrope
        Emerald
        Dark rose pink
        Dark jade
        Lt. green
        Black

WEFT: 4 fine yarns of the same color on the bobbin
        1 warp yarn
        3 wool 7/1 or worsted 20/2

WARP ENDS: 506

ENDS PER INCH: 27

REED: 12

WIDTH IN REED: 18″ + 5 dents

DENTING:
5 dents @ 4 per dent
7 dents @ 1 per dent
Repeat 18 times plus 5 dents @ 4 per dent

THREAD: 1, 2, 3, 4 with any color that comes up. The more mixed, the more interesting. End on H.2.

WARPING ORDER: No repeat in the warp order. Proportion of colors per one inch are:
5 blue
5 violet
4 heliotrope
4 emerald
3 lt. green
3 rose pink
2 jade
1 black

TREADLING: 1, 2
  2½″ blue
  1½″ emerald
  2½″ rose pink
  ¼″ violet
 *1½″ heliotrope
  ½″ blue
  1″ lt. green
  ½″ rose pink
*2½″ violet
  ¼″ heliotrope
  1½″ blue
  ½″ emerald
  1½″ rose pink
3″ violet—repeat from here in reverse.

TABLE LOOMS:
Levers: 1 + 3
       2 + 4
May be woven on the same warp as on page 65.

*Shown in photo

PILLOW

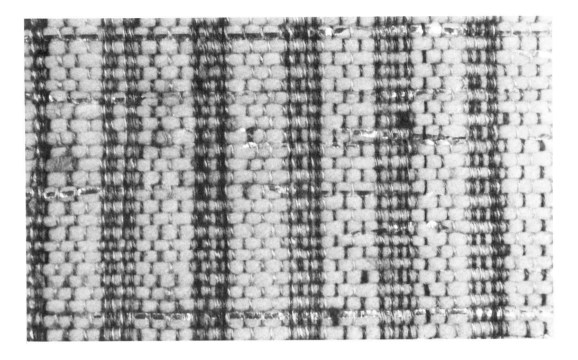

THREADING   TIE-UP

2 1

PLAIN WEAVE

WARP: 20/2 mercerized pearl cotton
      Skipper blue
      Violet
      Heliotrope
      Emerald
      Dark rose pink
      Dark jade
      Lt. green
      Black

WEFT: 4 ply cerise knitting yarn
Optional—$\frac{1}{16}''$ gold in same shed with yarn at random, about every fifth shot.

WARP ENDS: 506

ENDS PER INCH: 27

REED: 12

WIDTH IN REED: 18″ + 5 dents

DENTING:
5 dents @ 4 per dent
7 dents @ 1 per dent
Repeat 18 times plus 5 dents @ 4 per dent

THREAD: 1, 2, 3, 4 with any color that comes up—the more mixed, the more interesting. End on H.2.

WARPING ORDER: No repeat in the warp order. Proportion of colors per one inch are:
5 blue
5 violet
4 heliotrope
4 emerald
3 lt. green
3 rose pink
2 jade
1 black

TREADLING: 1, 2

TABLE LOOMS:
Levers: 1 + 3
      2 + 4
May be woven on the same warp as on page 64.

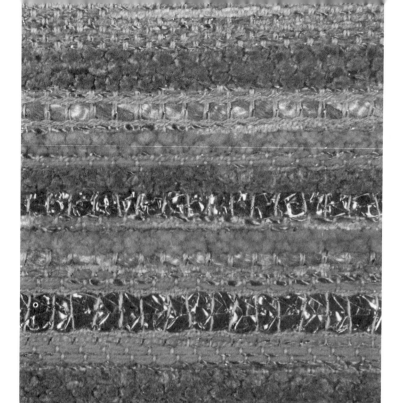

PILLOW 4 harness, 6 pedal

THREADING TIE-UP

6 5 4 3 2 1

WARP: Unmercerized linen color 10/2 cotton

WEFT:

Ground:
1 variegated tan 12 cut rayon chenille ⎫
1 tan-gold twist linen ⎬ Wound together
1 tan spun rayon ⎭

Group:
2 tan fingering wool ⎫
1 tan spun rayon ⎪ Wound together
1 tan-gold twist linen ⎬
1 linen color pearl 5 ⎭
Viscose and jute @ 140 yds. per lb.
Linen color pearl 5
Beige 6 cut cotton chenille
Lt. brown 3 cut rayon chenille
⅜″ gold braid
¼″ copper braid

WARP ENDS: 300

ENDS PER INCH: 15

REED: 15

WIDTH IN REED: 20″

DENTING: 1 per dent

THREAD: 1, 2, 3, 4

TREADLING:
4½″ ground 1, 2
3 brown chenille 3, 5, 3 ⎫
3 ground 2, 1, 2
3 group 4, 3, 6
3 pearl 1, 2, 1
1 gold braid 5
3 pearl 1, 2, 1
1 group 5
2 ground 1, 2
1 viscose 1
1 pearl 2
2 beige chenille 3, 5
1 pearl 1
3 ground 2, 1, 2
1 copper braid 3 ⎬ ×3
2 pearl 2, 1
2 brown chenille 5, 3
2 group 6, 5
1 pearl 1
2 beige chenille 5, 3
2 pearl 2, 1
1 group 5
3 pearl 1, 2, 1
1 viscose 2
3 pearl 1, 2, 1
2 ground 2, 1 ⎭
3 brown chenille 5, 3, 5
23″ ground 1, 2

TABLE LOOMS:
For pedal 1 use levers 3 + 4
For pedal 2 use levers 1 + 2
For pedal 3 use lever 4
For pedal 4 use lever 3
For pedal 5 use lever 2
For pedal 6 use lever 1

DECORATIVE FABRICS

Decorative fabrics for the most part are woven of such unusual yarns, both as to color and texture, that the simplest weaves will suffice, the yarns themselves being a characteristic part of the design.

There are many uses for decorative fabrics, some of which are listed along with the instructions for weaving. The weaver will undoubtedly think of other ways in which to use the fabrics for such articles as hand bags, evening skirts, boleros, tote bags and small accessories such as glass cases and coin purses. Some patterns may furnish inspiration for wall hangings, room dividers and screen panels.

In choosing a design, consideration is taken of other furnishings in the room, and of equal importance, the purpose of the fabric. In general, draperies should fall in soft folds, upholstery fabric should be firm, and spreads for bed or couch should be firm, but pliable.

It is doubtful if the colors given will suit everyone's needs. If the same effect is wanted, but other colors are used, plan them so that the values will fall into the same general scheme, with the darkest and lightest shades used in the same amounts and placement as given in the pattern. When choosing colors, always consider the effect weft colors will have both on each other, and woven against the warp color.

The yarns for each design are listed with their yardages, not so much as a guide for using the same yarns, but as a means of identifying them as to size and type, so that available similar yarns, either those on hand, or other suitable yarns for individual projects, may be substituted.

Since the selvages will be removed from these fabrics, it is not important, or even possible to make them neat. Heavy wefts will be carried up the sides, and need not be fastened back into the web in the usual way. It is best to cut them an inch or so beyond the selvage, and enter the new weft in the next shed, leaving an inch protruding. Braids and such are cut the width of the warp plus 2", taped to a shuttle, and shot across.

Metallics have been used in some of the patterns. For a time, the manufacturers made the use of metallics in handweaves undesirable. Handweavers had been using them sparingly with taste when the fabric lent itself to their use. Manufacturers, always with an eye on handweavers and their original ideas, picked up the metallic idea, and apparently on the assumption that if a glint was good, a glitter was better, they drenched everything in gold until finally we had metallic-shot wash cloths. Mass production depends on the new, and since there was nothing left without metallics, seemingly overnight, gold was out of vogue for mass-produced items. By now, however, it has been long enough so that handweavers may again add a bit of metallic where a sparkle is needed for an accent in some decorative fabrics.

HEADBOARD UPHOLSTERY

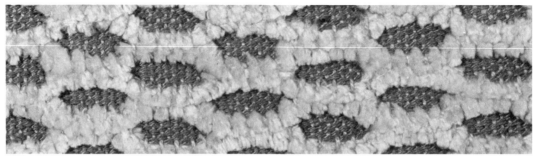

HONEYCOMB WEAVE

WARP: Natural 2 ply linen and rayon @ 2100 yds. per lb.

WEFT: Old gold color 2 ply linen and rayon @ 2100 yds. per lb.—doubled
Natural 3 cut rayon chenille @ 300 yds. per lb.

WARP ENDS: 440

ENDS PER INCH: 10

REED: 10

WIDTH IN REED: 44″

DENTING: 1 per dent

THREAD: Single in heddle
4, 3 ×5
2, 1 ×5

THREADING   TIE-UP

6 5 4 3 2 1

TREADLING:
1 chenille 1
8 doubled gold 3, 4 ×4
1 chenille 2
8 doubled gold 5, 6 ×4

TABLE LOOMS:
For pedal 1 use levers 1 + 3
For pedal 2 use levers 2 + 4
For pedal 3 use levers 1 + 2 + 3
For pedal 4 use levers 1 + 2 + 4
For pedal 5 use levers 1 + 3 + 4
For pedal 6 use levers 2 + 3 + 4
Bedspread woven on the same warp:
    Weft: 3 ply shiny cotton roving @ 400 yds. per lb. Tread: 1, 2

4 harness, 4 pedal

CURTAIN—BEDSPREAD FABRIC

THREADING TIE-UP

4 3 2 1

WARP: Unmercerized 10/2 linen color cotton @ 4200 yds. per lb.

WEFT: Variegated white—deep yellow rayon bouclé @ 2000 yds. per lb.

WARP ENDS: 1080

ENDS PER INCH: 24

REED: 12

WIDTH IN REED: 45″

DENTING: 2 per dent

THREAD: Single in heddle 1, 2, 3, 4

TREADLING: 1, 2, 3, 4
TABLE LOOMS:
For pedal 1 use lever 4
For pedal 2 use lever 3
For pedal 3 use lever 1
For pedal 4 use lever 2
REQUIREMENTS: For 1 yd.
Warp, 1080 yds.
Weft, 1170 yds.

DECORATIVE FABRICS

4 harness, 4 pedal

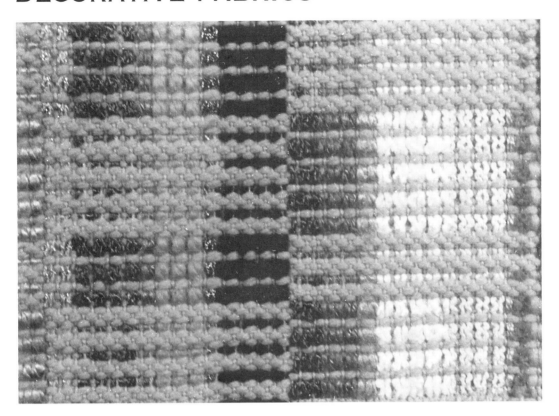

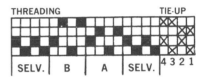

THREADING · TIE-UP

| SELV. | B | A | SELV. | 4 3 2 1 |

WARP PATTERN WEAVE

WARP:

Ground: Flame 8/2 cotton

Pattern: Cerise nylon-wool cable yarn
Melon 2 ply spun viscose
Persimmon-copper twist
Purple rayon bouclé
Fuchsia wool spun rayon
Mulberry nylon-wool cable yarn
Red braid
Black 8 cut chenille
Black pearl 3 cotton
White soft spun rayon ratine
Pink cotton ratine
Rose pearl 5, doubled
Red 8 cut chenille

WEFT: Flame 4 ply nylon-wool

WARP ENDS: 620 + 8 selv. = 628

ENDS PER INCH: 20

REED: 10

WIDTH IN REED: 31″ + 4 dents

DENTING: 2 per dent
(one end 8/2 + one pattern end)

THREAD: Single in heddle
Selv. 1, 2, 1, 2
BLOCK A Pattern 3
Ground 1
Pattern 3
Ground 2
BLOCK B Pattern 4
Ground 1
Pattern 4
Ground 2

WARPING ORDER: 4 flame selv.

NOTE—Warp one end flame 8/2 for every pattern end

BLOCK A
- 2 cerise
- 2 red chenille
- 1 rose, doubled
- 7 pink ratine
- 9 white ratine
- 2 melon
- 5 fuchsia
- 4 purple

BLOCK B
- 1 black pearl }
- 1 black chenille } ×4
- 1 red braid
- 3 mulberry
- 2 fuchsia
- 8 purple
- 4 persimmon

BLOCK A
- 3 melon
- 1 cerise

Repeat the whole 5 times + 4 flame selv.

TREADLING:

1, 2, 1, 4 ×3
1, 2, 1
4, 3, 4, 1 ×2
4, 3, 4
1, 2, 1, 4 ×4
1, 2, 1
4, 3, 4, 1 ×4
4, 3, 4

TABLE LOOMS:

For pedal 1 use levers 1 + 3
For pedal 2 use levers 2 + 3
For pedal 3 use levers 1 + 4
For pedal 4 use levers 2 + 4

Use two warp beams or heavy yarns, free hanging

USES: Short length upholstery for ottomans, benches, chair seats, pillows

4 harness, 2 pedal

WARP: Unmercerized 10/2 linen color cotton @ 4200 yds. per lb.

WEFT: Mustard wool, doubled. Norwegian Ullspissgarn @ approx. 640 yds. per lb.
Linen color heavy cotton nub @ 500 yds. per lb.

WARP ENDS: 660
ENDS PER INCH: 15
REED: 15
WIDTH IN REED: 44″
DENTING: 1 per dent

THREADING   TIE-UP

2 1

THREAD: Single in heddle 1, 2, 3, 4
TREADLING: 1, 2
2 shots doubled wool
1 shot doubled wool + cotton nub
Repeat

TABLE LOOMS:
Levers: 1 + 2
3 + 4

Reversible fabric. Needs no side hems.

USES: Couch throws, unlined insulation drapes

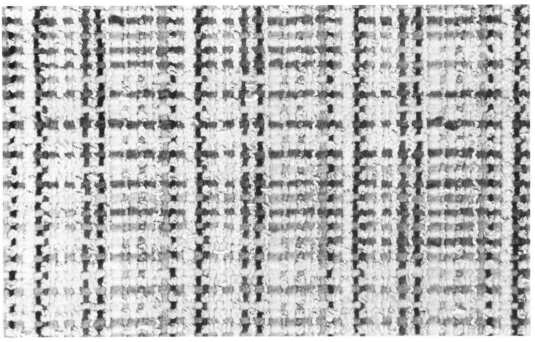

4 harness, 2 pedal

PLAIN WEAVE

WARP:
Pearl 3 mercerized cotton
    Natural
    Black
    Taupe
    Dk. olive
8/4 carpet warp
    Natural
    Black
12/4 lt. olive cotton
Natural cotton rug yarn
Natural rayon ratine

WEFT:
Natural rayon ratine ⎫ Wound
Natural rayon nub ⎬ together
Variegated white-grey-tan wool spun rayon
    @ 960 yds. per lb.

WARP ENDS: 440

ENDS PER INCH: 10

REED: 10

WIDTH IN REED: 44″

DENTING: 1 per dent

THREAD: Single in heddle 1, 2, 3, 4 in the
    same order as warping order

WARPING ORDER: One end of each yarn
Black carpet warp
Rug yarn
Natural pearl
Black pearl
Lt. olive
Ratine
Natural carpet warp
Taupe
Natural pearl
Lt. olive
Rug yarn
Natural carpet warp
Black pearl
Ratine
Dk. olive
Natural carpet warp ⎫
Natural pearl   ⎬ ×2
Dk. olive

THREADING TIE-UP

2 1

TREADLING: 1, 2
1 variegated
1 ratine + nub
Repeat

TABLE LOOMS:
Levers: 1 + 3
       2 + 4

USES: Couch covers, upholstery, drapes

TREADLING: 9″ repeat

24 ground 4 + 1, 1 + 2, 2 + 3,
    3 + 4 ×6
*4 yellow 2, 3, 4, 1
 3 ground 6, 5, 6
 2 aqua 1, 2
 2 ground 5, 6
 8 aqua 1, 2, 3, 4 ×2
 2 ground 5, 6
12 aqua 1, 2, 3, 4 ×3
 3 ground 5, 6, 5
 4 black 2, 3, 4, 1
 3 ground 6, 5, 6
 4 aqua 1, 2, 3, 4
 2 ground 5, 6
 4 yellow 1, 2, 3, 4
 2 ground 5, 6
12 aqua 1, 2, 3, 4 ×3
*3 ground 5, 6, 5
 8 aqua 2, 3, 4, 1
 2 ground 6, 5
 2 rust 2, 3
 2 ground 6, 5
 2 rust 2, 3
24 ground 1 + 2, 2 + 3, 3 + 4,
    4 + 1 ×6
 2 antique 1 + 2, 2 + 3 ⎤
 2 ground 3 + 4, 4 + 1 ⎦ ×3
 2 antique 1 + 2, 2 + 3
 1 ground 3 + 4
Repeat

TABLE LOOMS:
For pedal 1 use lever 4
For pedal 2 use lever 3
For pedal 3 use lever 2
For pedal 4 use lever 1
For pedal 5 use levers 2 + 4
For pedal 6 use levers 1 + 3

USES: Upholstery, drapes,
  floor pillows
*Shown in photo

THREADING TIE-UP

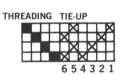

6 5 4 3 2 1

WARP: Ecru 5/2 cotton
WEFT:
Ground: Natural jute and rayon @ 1200
  yds. per lb.
Pattern: Slub rayon @ 840 yds. per lb.
    Canary yellow
    Aqua
    Black
    Rust
    Antique gold
WARP ENDS: 660
ENDS PER INCH: 15
REED: 15
WIDTH IN REED: 44″
DENTING: 1 per dent
THREAD: Single in heddle 1, 2, 3, 4.

DECORATIVE FABRICS

4 harness, 2 pedal

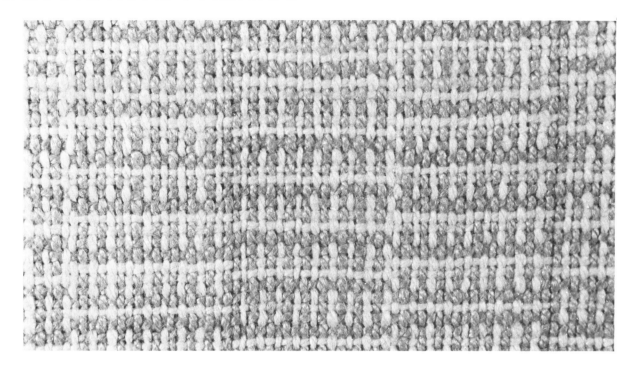

THREADING TIE-UP

2 1

WARPING ORDER:

1 natural
1 tan } ×9

1 tan
1 natural } ×9

TREADLING: 1, 2

1 shot eggshell
1 shot tan } ×2

1 shot eggshell
2 shot tan } ×3

2 shot eggshell
1 shot tan } ×2

2 shot eggshell
2 shot tan } ×4

TABLE LOOMS:

For pedal 1 use levers 1 + 3
For pedal 2 use levers 2 + 4

USES: Unlined curtains, couch covers

LOG CABIN WEAVE

WARP: Natural heavy 4/4 carpet warp
@ 400 yds. per 8 oz. tube
Tan wool spun rayon @ 960 yds.
per lb.

WEFT: Eggshell soft twist 4/4 filler
Tan wool spun rayon

WARP ENDS: 540

ENDS PER INCH: 12

REED: 12

WIDTH IN REED: 45″

DENTING: 1 per dent

THREAD: Single in heddle 1, 2, 3, 4

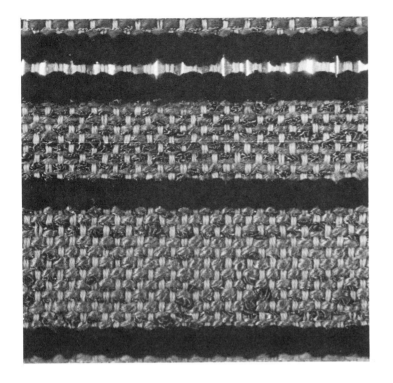

WARP: 8/2 flame cotton @ 3360 yds. per lb.

WEFT:

Black 6 cut cotton chenille

3/16" metallic flatfold
>Red
>Blue
>Green gold

Cotton roving
>Bright rose
>Persian blue

Shiny cotton
>Emerald
>Yellow

Rayon bouclé
>Turquoise
>Purple, doubled
>Emerald
>Variegated yellow-white

8/2 bright rose rayon

WARP ENDS: 660

ENDS PER INCH: 15

REED: 15

WIDTH IN REED: 44"

DENTING: 1 per dent

THREAD: Single in heddle 1, 2, 3, 4

May be woven on the same warp as on page 75.

THREADING   TIE-UP

4 3 2 1

(74)

TREADLING:

*8 inches rose (roving + 8/2 rayon) 1, 2
3 black 3, 4, 3
12 green (shiny cotton + green bouclé)
2, 1 ×6
3 black 4, 3, 4
10 purple (double bouclé + fuchsia)
1, 2 ×5
3 black 3, 4, 3
1 gold fold 2
3 black 3, 4, 3
*12 blue (roving + turq. bouclé) 2, 1 ×6
3 black 4, 3, 4
16 rose 1, 2 ×8
3 black 3, 4, 3
1 blue fold 2
3 black 3, 4, 3
14 yellow (shiny cotton + variegated
bouclé) 2, 1 ×7
3 black 4, 3, 4
8 green 1, 2 ×4
3 black 3, 4, 3
1 red fold 2
3 black 3, 4, 3
18 blue 2, 1 ×9
3 black 4, 3, 4
6 purple 1, 2 ×3
3 black 3, 4, 3
1 gold 2
3 black 3, 4, 3
14 green 2, 1 ×7
2 black 4, 3, 4
10 rose 1, 2 ×5
3 black 3, 4, 3
1 red fold 2
3 black 3, 4, 3
8 yellow 2, 1 ×4
3 black 4, 3, 4
1 blue fold 1
3 black 4, 3, 4
3 blue 1, 2, 1
3 black 4, 3, 4

Rose 1, 2 for remainder of panel

TABLE LOOMS:

For pedal 1 use levers 1 + 2
For pedal 2 use levers 3 + 4
For pedal 3 use lever 2
For pedal 4 use lever 4

*Shown in photo

WARP: 8/2 flame cotton @ 3360 yds. per lb.

WEFT: Shiny cotton @ 400 yds. per lb.
        Bronze green   Yellow
        Emerald
    Cotton roving @ 600 yds. per lb.
        Bright rose   Royal
    3/16" metallic flatfold
        Red   Green-gold
        Blue
    Rayon bouclé
        Emerald
        Purple, doubled
        Old gold color, doubled
        Variegated yellow-white
    Chenille
        Yellow rayon 8 cut, doubled
        Olive cotton 6 cut
    Natural jute and rayon twist
        @ 140 yds. per lb.
    Fuchsia wool spun rayon
    Bright rose 8/2 rayon

TREADLING: for 3 yards

18 inches bronze 1, 2
2 rose (roving + 8/2 rayon) 1, 2
1 red fold 1
2 rose 2, 1
1 purple (bouclé doubled + 1 fuchsia) 2
2 rose 1, 2
1 red fold 1
2 rose 2, 1
1 yellow doubled chenille 2
4 rose 1, 2, 1, 2
2 blue roving 1, 3
2 green 2, 4
*1 yellow doubled chenille 1
2 gold doubled bouclé 2, 1
2 olive chenille 2, 1
1 blue fold 2
2 olive chenille 1, 2
1 jute and rayon 1
2 rose 2, 1
2 purple 2, 1
2 rose 2, 1
2 yellow doubled chenille 2, 1
1 gold fold 2
2 yellow doubled chenille 1, 2
1 bronze 1
4 yellow (shiny + yellow-white bouclé)
    3, 2, 4, 1
*1 rose 2

4 harness, 4 pedal

2 green 1, 2
2 rose 1, 2
1 purple 1
4 inches bronze 2, 1
2 rose 2, 1
1 red fold 2
2 rose 1, 2
2 purple 1, 2
2 rose 1, 2
1 yellow doubled chenille 1
1 gold fold 2
1 yellow doubled chenille 1
1 rose 1
3 green 3, 2, 4
1 blue 1
1 rose 2
6 inches bronze 1, 2
3 purple 1, 2, 1
1 rose 2
3 green 1, 3, 2
1 blue 4
2 rose 1, 2
6 inches bronze 1, 2
2 rose 1, 2
4 bronze 1, 2, 1, 2
2 rose 1, 2
2 yards bronze 1, 2

THREADING TIE-UP

4 3 2 1

TABLE LOOMS:

For pedal 1 use levers 3 + 4
For pedal 2 use levers 1 + 2
For pedal 3 use levers 2 + 3
For pedal 4 use levers 1 + 4
Drapery length, 3 yards, may be woven on
    the same warp as on page 74.

*Shown in photo

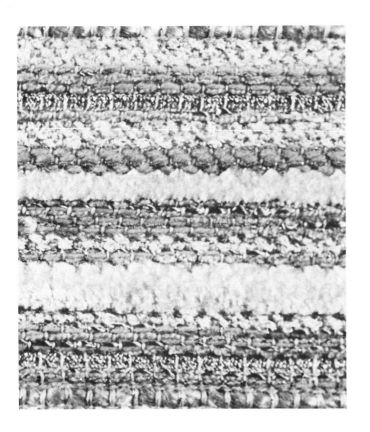

WARP ENDS: 660
ENDS PER INCH: 15
REED: 15
WIDTH IN REED: 44″
DENTING: 1 per dent
THREAD: Single in heddle 1, 2, 3, 4
TREADLING: 4″ repeat
4 natural group 1, 2, 1, 2
1 silk 1
1 viscose 2
3 silk 1, 2, 1
1 beige group 5
1 silk 1
1 straw 6
3 beige 4, 5, 6
2 natural 1, 2
3 chenille 3, 5, 3
3 silk 2, 1, 2
1 beige 3
2 natural 2, 1
4 beige 5, 6, 3, 4
2 chenille 6, 4
3 butterscotch 6, 3, 4
3 natural 2, 1, 2
1 beige 3
1 straw 5
1 silk 3
3 beige 4, 5, 6
Repeat

TABLE LOOMS:
For pedal 1 use levers 1 + 2
For pedal 2 use levers 3 + 4
For pedal 3 use lever 1
For pedal 4 use lever 2
For pedal 5 use lever 3
For pedal 6 use lever 4

USES: Decorative coverlets, headboard up-holstery, bands in drapes, bench up-holstery, pillows

THREADING   TIE-UP

6 5 4 3 2 1

WARP: Natural 20/2 linen @ 3000 yds. per lb.

WEFT:
Natural color group
    1 rayon ratine
    1 soft spun rayon ratine } Wound together
    1 rayon nub
Beige group
    1 fine rayon bouclé
    1 rayon 12 cut chenille } Wound together
    1 silk twist
    2 botany wool
Butterscotch group
    1 fine rayon bouclé
    2 worsted 20/2 } Wound together
    1 knitting yarn 4 ply
Heavy viscose and jute twist
Natural rayon 3 cut chenille.
³⁄₁₆″ pale yellow straw braid
Natural silk twist

DECORATIVE FABRICS

4 harness, 6 pedal

TREADLING: 18" repeat
*5 inches lt. red + orange 1, 2
2 med. yellow 1, 2
1 green gold 1
2 med. yellow 2, 1
1 lt. red + orange 2
2 med. yellow 1, 2
1 pale yellow 1
2 med. yellow 2, 1
2 lt. red + orange 2, 1
4 pale yellow 6, 5, 4, 3
1 med. yellow 2
2 lt. red + orange 1, 2
1 doubled chenille 1
1 lt. red + orange 2
1 doubled chenille 1
1 gold 2
1 doubled chenille 1
1 lt. red + orange 2
1 doubled chenille 1
2 lt. red + orange 2, 1
4 med. yellow 5, 6, 3, 4
1 pale yellow 5
*5 inches lt. red + orange 1, 2
2 pale yellow 3, 4
4 med. yellow 5, 6, 3, 4
4 inches lt. red + orange

TABLE LOOMS:
For pedal 1 use levers 3 + 4
For pedal 2 use levers 1 + 2
For pedal 3 use lever 4
For pedal 4 use lever 3
For pedal 5 use lever 2
For pedal 6 use lever 1

USES: Drapes, coverlets, pillows

*Shown in photo

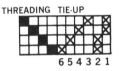

THREADING TIE-UP

6 5 4 3 2 1

WARP: 8/2 lt. red cotton @ 3360 yds. per lb.

WEFT: Soft spun rayon ratine
Lt. red ⎱ Wound
Orange ⎰ together
3 ply shiny cotton @ 400 yds. per lb.
Pale yellow
Med. yellow
3/16" metallic fold
Gold
Green gold
Yellow 8 cut cotton chenille, doubled

WARP ENDS: 672

ENDS PER INCH: 15

REED: 15

WIDTH IN REED: 45" less 3 dents

DENTING: 1 per dent

THREAD: Single in heddle 1, 2, 3, 4

(77)

BEDSPREAD 82" x 113"

PLAIN WEAVE

WARP:
Pearl 3 cotton
    Beige
    Natural
    3 shades of any one color: dark, medium, light
Natural 8/4 carpet warp
Natural rayon ratine
Eggshell 4/4 soft twist cotton

WEFT:
Natural rayon bouclé ⎫ Wound
Natural rayon knot   ⎬ together
Eggshell 4/4 same as warp

WARP ENDS: 440

ENDS PER INCH: 10

REED: 10

WIDTH IN REED: 44"

DENTING: 1 per dent

THREAD: Single in heddle 1, 2, 3, 4

To make: Cut fabric in half. Cut one piece in half lengthwise. Sew these two to either side of wider piece. Adjust to 39" wide for center panel. Welting optional. Hem top and bottom.

WARPING ORDER: One end of each yarn
Carpet warp
Natural pearl
Med. color
Ratine
Darkest color
Carpet warp
Eggshell
Lightest color
Carpet warp
Beige
Carpet warp
Ratine
Light
Dark
Natural pearl
Eggshell
Dark
Medium
Carpet warp
Natural pearl

THREADING TIE-UP

2 1

TREADLING: Bouclé + knot 1, 2, 1
              Eggshell 2

TABLE LOOMS:
For pedal 1 use levers 1 + 3
For pedal 2 use levers 2 + 4

REQUIREMENTS: 8 yd. warp includes take-up, waste and hems

ЭECORATIVE FABRICS

4 harness, 4 pedal

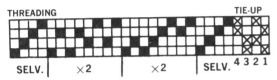

4 harness, 5 pedal

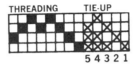

M'S AND O'S

WARP: Natural soft spun 12/3 cotton @ 3360 yds. per lb.

WEFT: Natural soft spun rayon ratine @ 800 yds. per lb.

WARP ENDS: 1056 + 8 selv. = 1064

ENDS PER INCH: 24

REED: 12

WIDTH IN REED: 44″ + 4 dents

DENTING: 2 per dent

THREAD: Single in heddle

Selv. 4, 3, 2, 1
4, 3, 4, 3, 2, 1, 2, 1 ×2
4, 2, 4, 2, 3, 1, 3, 1 ×2
Selv. 4, 3, 2, 1

TREADLING:

1, 2 ×4
3, 4 ×4

TABLE LOOMS:

Levers: 1 + 3 ⎫ ×4
   2 + 4 ⎭
   1 + 2 ⎫ ×4
   3 + 4 ⎭

Yardage for a complete room may be woven of this fabric.
  Upholstery—Piece dyed in muted colors
  Curtains—Left natural
  Pillows—Piece dyed in bright colors

WAFFLE WEAVE

WARP: 8/2 flame soft spun cotton @ 3360 yds. per lb.

WEFT: 8/2 flame cotton same as warp
   Flame soft spun rayon ratine

WARP ENDS: 864

ENDS PER INCH: 24

REED: 12

WIDTH IN REED: 36″

DENTING: 2 per dent

THREAD: Single in heddle
1, 2, 3, 4, 3, 4, 3, 2

TREADLING:

 5 cotton 3, 4, 5, 4, 3
 3 rayon 2, 1, 2
 5 cotton 3, 4, 5, 4, 3
11 rayon 2, 1, 2, 3, 4, 5, 4, 3, 2, 1, 2
Repeat

TABLE LOOMS:

For pedal 1 use lever 1
For pedal 2 use lever 2
For pedal 3 use levers 1 + 3
For pedal 4 use levers 1 + 2 + 4
For pedal 5 use levers 1 + 2 + 3

USES: Bedspreads, coverlets, pillows.
(In 12/2 wool—blankets)

DECORATIVE FABRICS

4 harness, 4 pedal

THREADING TIE-UP

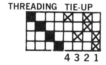

4 3 2 1

WARP: Natural 14/2 linen @ 2100 yds.
WEFT:
Wool spun rayon @ 960 yds. per lb.
    Tan, tripled on bobbin
    Lt. olive, doubled
    Olive, doubled
    Antique, doubled
Dk. brown 8 cut chenille
Dk. brown 4 ply wool, doubled
WARP ENDS: 300
ENDS PER INCH: 15
REED: 15
WIDTH IN REED: 20″
DENTING: 1 per dent
THREAD: Single in heddle 1, 2, 3, 4

TREADLING: 1, 2 except chenille and wool
  as indicated
  4 antique
  4 lt. olive
  4 antique
  1 tan
  2 antique
  1 tan
  4 antique
  1 tan
  2 antique
  2 olive   } ×2
  2 antique
  3 chenille—tread 4, 3, 4
14 antique
  1 tan   } ×3
  2 antique
  2 chenille—tread 4, 3
  2 antique
  2 wool—tread 4, 3
  2 antique
  3 wool—tread 4, 3, 4
  6 antique

TABLE LOOMS:
For pedal 1 use levers 1 + 2
For pedal 2 use levers 3 + 4
For pedal 3 use lever 2
For pedal 4 use lever 4
Chair seat fabric, upholster with stripes
  running from front to back

4 harness, 6 pedal

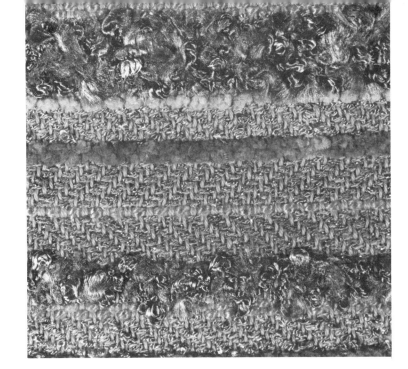

TREADLING: 14" repeat
 4 melon 3, 1, 3, 1
 5 putty 5, 6, 5, 6, 5
*8 bronze 1, 2, 3, 4 ×2
 2 melon 2, 4
 3 green 5, 6, 5
 8 bronze 1, 2, 3, 4 ×2
 1 melon 2
 8 bronze 4, 3, 2, 1 ×2
 3 putty 5, 6, 5
 8 bronze 1, 2, 3, 4 ×2
 1 chartreuse 5
 1 melon 1
 6 green 5, 6 ×3
 2 bronze 3, 1
*4 melon 3, 1 ×2
 4 bronze 4, 3, 2, 1
 2 melon 3, 1
 5 putty 5, 6, 5, 6, 5
 4 bronze 4, 3, 2, 1
 4 melon 3, 1 ×2
12 green 5, 6 ×6 (center)
Repeat in reverse, 4 melon etc.

TABLE LOOMS:
For pedal 1 use levers 1 + 2
For pedal 2 use levers 2 + 3
For pedal 3 use levers 3 + 4
For pedal 4 use levers 1 + 4
For pedal 5 use lever 3
For pedal 6 use lever 1

USES: Bedspreads, Coverlets, Drapes, Chair seats, Bench upholstery, Pillows

*Shown in photo

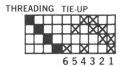

THREADING   TIE-UP

6 5 4 3 2 1

WARP: Melon 8/2 soft twist cotton @ 3360
 yds. per lb.
WEFT:
Melon shiny cotton @ 400 yds.
6 cut cotton chenille
    Putty
    Chartreuse
Green rayon loop fringe bouclé @ 450 yds.
 per lb., doubled
Bronze rayon bouclé @ 1700 yds. per lb.,
 doubled
WARP ENDS: 672 for 45" reed or
            540 for 36" reed
ENDS PER INCH: 15
REED: 15
WIDTH IN REED: 45" less 3 dents or
                36"
DENTING: 1 per dent
THREAD: Single in heddle 1, 2, 3, 4

(81)

DECORATIVE FABRIC

4 harness, 4 pedal

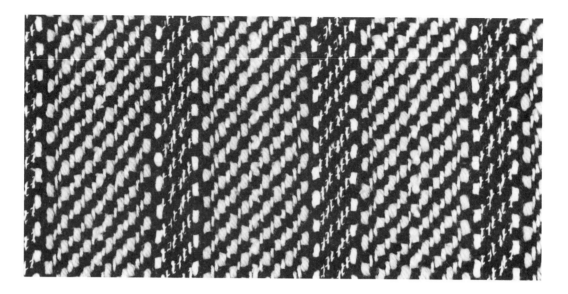

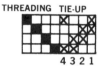

4 3 2 1

TWILL

WARP: 4/4 carpet warp
        Natural
        Mustard
      Black 8/4 carpet warp
      Yellow pearl 3
      Yellow heavy cotton novelty
      Chartreuse 12/4 cotton
      Black and white twist

WEFT: Black cotton ratine

WARP ENDS: 616

ENDS PER INCH: 14

REED: 15

WIDTH IN REED: 44" less one dent

DENTING: 1 per dent for 27 dents
        1 empty dent
        1 yellow novelty per dent
        1 empty dent

THREAD: Single in heddle
1, 2, 3, 4 in same order as warping order
Substitute carpet warp for last end on left
   selvage side

WARPING ORDER:
1 chartreuse ⎫
1 mustard   ⎬ ×2
1 yellow pearl
1 mustard
2 chartreuse
1 mustard
1 black
1 natural
6 black and white
1 black
1 mustard
2 chartreuse
1 mustard
1 yellow pearl
1 mustard   ⎫
1 chartreuse ⎬ ×2
1 yellow novelty

TREADLING: 1, 2, 3, 4

TABLE LOOMS:
For pedal 1 use levers 3 + 4
For pedal 2 use levers 2 + 3
For pedal 3 use levers 1 + 2
For pedal 4 use levers 1 + 4

USES: Reversible throws, unlined drapes

RUGS

The first requirement for rug weaving is a strong, sturdy loom, although it need not necessarily be a "rug loom." Any sturdy loom will weave rugs if the beater is heavy enough. A heavy metal handle attached to the beater or a supplementary beater will give the weight needed.

Linen is considered the best rug warp, and must certainly be used for rugs with wool weft to give the rug weight and durability. Great care must always be taken in the beaming of linen because of its non-elastic character. This is especially true of a linen rug warp. Only a well-tensioned warp will produce a rug that will lie flat on the floor.

For washable rugs with cotton filler, rags, or roving, use a cotton carpet warp of good quality.

Weft of wool or cotton is shuttled in the shed loosely at an angle. Two sharp beats are needed to make a firm rug.

Selvages are reinforced by doubling warp ends on either side. Heddle them in the same heddles on the same frame, and double dent the two ends.

Width shrinkage is from 2" to 3", depending on the type materials used. Since most of the shrinkage occurs at the selvage sides, it will be about the same amount for widths from 27" to 36", and even 42".

To weave the length wanted, take-up will be found by measuring 10" or 12" on the loom, loosening the tension and measuring again. Compare measurements. Use this as a guide for further measuring.

Other measurements which should be made as weaving progresses are rug width and number of picks per inch. All should be checked often to keep the weaving uniform.

Of all the rug techniques, probably the one in which the most interest is shown is the Scandinavian Rya. There are many imported kits available which contain finished woven background mats, yarns, and necessary equipment along with a pattern, and they do make up into beautiful rugs. There is, however, great satisfaction in weaving the complete rug, and in any size or proportion wanted.

As in all weaving, consideration for the colors in the room will be taken into account, also the floor space the rug is to occupy and its relation to other furnishings. The long, narrow rug is a good choice for a sofa. To weave the rug sofa length and as wide as the space between sofa and coffee table is practical and very decorative. This proportion is equally good in front of the fireplace and down the center of a narrow hall. Not too long a rug can be planned, however, because of the build-up on the cloth beam. Nevertheless, any width can be made by joining strips, concealing the joining with rya knots.

Rya rugs usually end in knotted

fringe, but another way to end a rya is to weave extra background at the beginning and end of the mat. This is turned back and finished with tape, either sewed or ironed on.

Choice of materials is most important. Only linen rug warp, strong, coarse wool for weaving, and fast wool or worsted for the knots should be used. Scandinavian notharsgarn, called cowhair, makes a good ground weaving yarn. It comes in many colors, although the only places the color will be seen is on the back and at the beginning and end of the rug. One-half inch of this is woven between rows of knots.

The yarns chosen for the knots may vary from dull wool to worsteds with high sheen. Mixing the two is often effective. The size of the yarns may also vary, using 2, 3, or even 4 strands together to build up uniform size. Although yarns may vary in size and type, they must be good rug yarns. Knitting yarns and other soft yarns, even of good quality, should not be used, as their very softness will result in a rug without spring.

To prepare the yarn for knots, cut through the skein and pull out a strand or strands needed for one knot, combining colors according to a selected pattern. Yarns are then threaded in a blunt 2½″

long rya needle, or made into butterflies. Good sharp scissors and a rya stick are needed. Some supply houses now carry the sticks, but one can be made with 2 very thin pieces of 1″ wide wood, put together with a thin piece of cardboard ¾″ wide between them. The ¼″ groove is for cutting.

Knots are cut either on the groove, giving straight ridges, or unevenly, giving a uniform, unevenly cut surface. To cut unevenly, cut a few strands just in front of the grooved edge, a few on the edge, and a few just behind it.

Yarn amounts will vary according to types used, width of rya stick, and number of shots between rows of knots. However, allow approximately 8 oz. of wool for 1 sq. ft. of knots. For true proportion, when making designs on squared paper, use 2 sqs. up, and one across, for each knot. This then is redrawn on regular squared paper, as a more convenient guide to work from. Allow 2 warp threads for each knot, plus two at either selvage side, which are left free to keep edges from rolling.

No matter what type rug you decide to weave, be it elaborate, or a simple rag rug, if care is taken in execution and in the choice of materials, you will have created a basic part of a room.

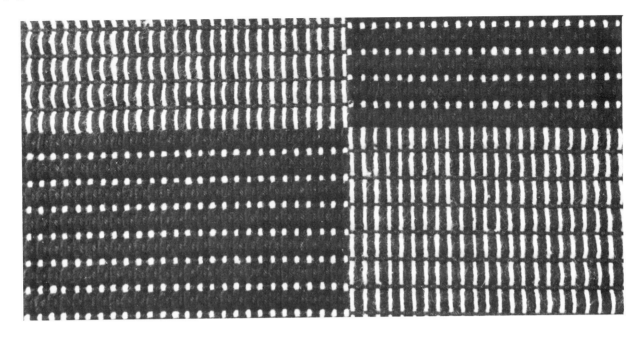

THREADING TIE-UP

2 1

LOG CABIN

WARP: 8/4 cotton carpet warp
Black
Natural

WEFT:

Rug #1: Heavy black rug filler @ 100 yds. per lb.
Black carpet warp

Rug #2: Heavy natural rug filler @ 100 yds. per lb.
Natural carpet warp

WARP ENDS: 420

ENDS PER INCH: 15

REED: 15

WIDTH IN REED: 28″

DENTING: 1 per dent

THREAD: Single in heddle

A $\left[\begin{array}{l}\text{Harness 1 black}\\\text{Harness 2 natural}\\\text{Harness 3 black}\\\text{Harness 4 natural}\end{array}\right\} \times 21$

B $\left[\begin{array}{l}\text{Harness 1 natural}\\\text{Harness 2 black}\\\text{Harness 3 natural}\\\text{Harness 4 black}\end{array}\right\} \times 21$

Thread A, B, A, B, A

WARPING ORDER:

A $\left\{\begin{array}{l}\text{1 black}\\\text{1 natural}\end{array}\right\} \times 42$

B $\left\{\begin{array}{l}\text{1 natural}\\\text{1 black}\end{array}\right\} \times 42$

Warp A, B, A, B, A

TREADLING: 1, 2

Start rug with 3 shots carpet warp

$\left.\begin{array}{l}\text{1 shot carpet warp}\\\text{1 shot rug filler}\end{array}\right\}$ weave 6″

1 shot rug filler

Repeat 9 times

4 shots carpet warp to end

Finish with knotted fringe, 6 ends per knot

TABLE LOOMS:

Levers: 1 + 3
2 + 4

REQUIREMENTS: For 2 rugs 26″ × 50″:
5 yd. warp
1 lb. black carpet warp
1 lb. natural carpet warp
2 lb. black rug filler
2 lb. natural rug filler

RYA RUG 19″ x 70″

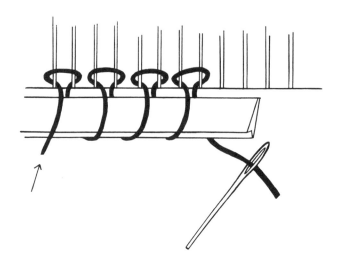

THREADING TIE-UP

2 1

WARP: Natural 8/3 linen rug warp @ 800 yds. per lb.

WEFT:

Background: Natural Swedish cowhair @ 600 yds. per lb.

Knots: Rug wool or worsted, various colors.

Threaded in needle: 1 heavy yarn + 1 medium heavy or 2 medium heavy yarns or 4 finer yarns.

WARP ENDS: 128

ENDS PER INCH: 6

REED: 6

WIDTH IN REED: 21″ + 2 dents

DENTING: 1 per dent

THREAD: Single in heddle 1, 2

TREADLING: 1, 2

Allow for fringe or weave for hems at start and end with cowhair.

Weave ½″ of single cowhair between every row of knots.

Knots: Work from left to right.

Leave first and last warp threads free.

Knots are made over 2 warp threads.

Knots are cut unevenly, a few strands are cut on the edge of the stick, a few just in front and a few just behind it.

REQUIREMENTS: 3½ yd. warp, 9 oz. linen

Cowhair, 4 lbs.

Rug yarn, 7 lbs.

Rya needles (2¾″, blunt)

Rya stick, approx. 1″ wide

RYA YARN

1. peacock and light blue
2. red, orange and burnt orange
3. medium blues
4. black and eggplant
5. cranberry, violet and magenta
6. black and royal
7. royal and green
8. light and medium grey
9. black and green
10. cerise, pink and rose
11. royal and light blue
12. black and purple
13. peacock and green
14. purples
15. rose and cyclamen
16. tangerine, orange and red
17. light and dark olive
18. black and brown heather
19. light and dark brown
20. light and medium purple
21. emerald and green
22. royal and peacock
23. medium and dark brown
24. orange and burnt orange
25. cerise and cranberry
26. black and magenta

Each sq. on the chart represents one knot.

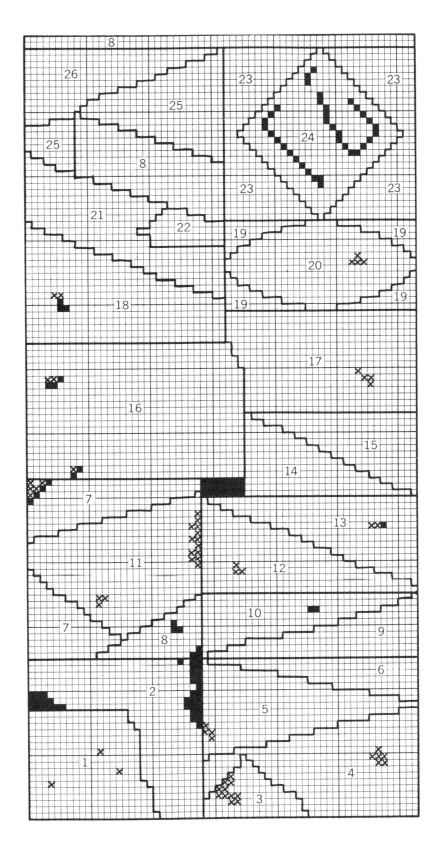

HIGHLIGHTS
DARK ACCENTS

RUG

20" x 36"

4 harness, 3 pedal

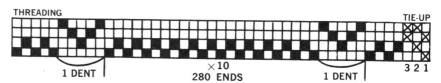

THREADING   TIE-UP

1 DENT   ×10   1 DENT   3 2 1

280 ENDS

CHENILLE WEAVE

WARP: Natural 8/4 carpet warp

WEFT: Rayon and cotton rug yarn @ 70
yds. per skein
         Turquoise
         Ivory

WARP ENDS: 294

REED: 12

WIDTH IN REED: 20½"

DENTING:
2 per dent twice
5 per dent once
1 per dent for 23 dents } ×10
5 per dent once
2 per dent twice
1 per dent once

THREAD: Single in heddle
2, 1 ×2
4, 3, 2, 3, 4
1, 2 ×11   } ×10
1
4, 3, 2, 3, 4
1, 2 ×2
1

TREADLING:
Carpet warp heading 1, 2, 1
Turquoise 2, 1, 2
40" {
     Ivory 3 (leave 1" loop at side)
     Turquoise 1
     Ivory 3 (leave 1" loop at side)
     Turquoise 2
Turquoise 1, 2, 1
Carpet warp 2, 1, 2
Knot fringe at 4 ends per knot
Cut through center of ivory floats
Cut through loops and trim

TABLE LOOMS:
For pedal 1 use levers 1 + 3
For pedal 2 use levers 2 + 4
For pedal 3 use levers 3 + 4

REQUIREMENTS: 2½ yd. warp includes
loom allowance, fringe and take-up.
½ lb. carpet warp
3 skeins turquoise
3 skeins ivory

(88)

RAG RUG 25" x 50"

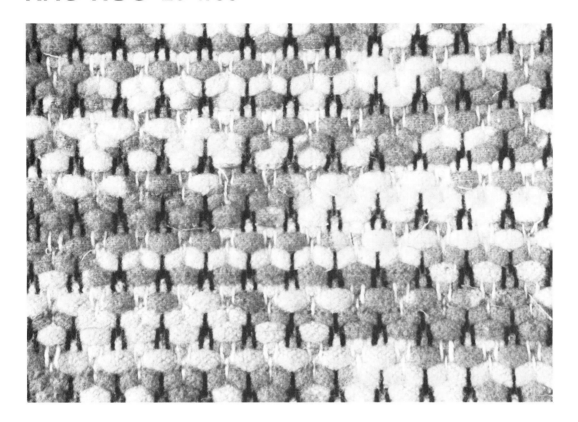

THREADING TIE-UP

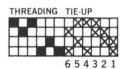

6 5 4 3 2 1

DOUBLE SEED

WARP: 8/4 cotton carpet warp
     Black
     Natural

WEFT: Cotton flannel sheeting cut into
  1½" strips
Colors in sheeting: Rose, pink, blue, green
  and natural, plaid

WARP ENDS: 324

ENDS PER INCH: 12

REED: 12

WIDTH IN REED: 27"

DENTING: 1 per dent

THREAD: Single in heddle
Black 1, 2, 1
Natural 4, 3, 4

WARPING ORDER:
3 black
3 natural

TREADLING: 1, 2, 3, 4
4 shots carpet warp at start and end
  5, 6 ×2

TABLE LOOMS:
Levers: 1 + 2
       2 + 3
       3 + 4
       1 + 4
4 shots carpet warp at start and end
  2 + 4 ⎫
  1 + 3 ⎭ ×2

REQUIREMENTS: 3 yd. warp
  6 oz. black
  6 oz. natural
  2 lbs. sheeting

WOOL RUG 34" x 50"

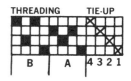

THREADING   TIE-UP

B   A   4 3 2 1

DOUBLE FACE

WARP: Natural 8/4 linen carpet warp @ 600 yds. per lb.

WEFT: Doubled Norwegian "Ullspissgarn" @ 640 yds. per lb.
  Natural
  Lt. grey
  Mustard yellow

WARP ENDS: 384

ENDS PER INCH: 10

REED: 10

WIDTH IN REED: 38" + 3 dents

DENTING: 2 per dent
1 empty dent

THREAD: Two per heddle
A block 1, 3, 2, 3
B block 1, 4, 2, 4
Thread block A ×6
         B ×20
         A ×6
         B ×40
         A ×6
         B ×12
         A ×6

REQUIREMENTS: 3 yd. warp
2 lbs. linen warp
3 lbs. wool, one lb. each color

TREADLING:

A
```
2
2 + 3 + 4
1
1 + 3 + 4
```

B
```
2 + 3
2 + 4
1 + 3
1 + 4
```

Start and end with 4 shots linen tabby

TABBY
```
1 + 2
3 + 4
```

Doubled weft

A ×4 (16 shots)	Natural Grey Natural Grey
B 6 inches	Yellow Natural Yellow Natural
A ×8	Natural Natural Natural Natural
B 3 inches	Grey Yellow Grey Yellow
A ×4	Natural Grey Natural Grey
B 4 inches	Yellow Natural Yellow Natural
A ×4	Natural Natural Natural Natural
A ×4	Natural Yellow Natural Yellow
A ×4	Grey Yellow Grey Yellow
B 5 inches	Natural Grey Natural Grey

A ×12	Natural Natural Natural Natural
A ×4	Yellow Natural Yellow Natural
B 8 inches	Grey Yellow Grey Yellow
A ×4	Natural Natural Natural Natural
B 3 inches	Grey Yellow Grey Yellow
A ×8	Natural Natural Natural Natural
B 4 inches	Grey Yellow Grey Yellow
A ×4	Natural Grey Natural Grey
B 9 inches	Yellow Natural Yellow Natural
A ×4	Natural Grey Natural Grey

RUG 40" x 72"

4 harness, 4 pedal

THREADING TIE-UP

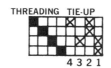

4 3 2 1

TREADLING:
8 jute 1, 2 ×4
1 carpet warp 3
1 chenille 4
1 carpet warp 3
8 jute 2, 1 ×4
1 multiple yarns 4
3 jute 1, 2, 1
1 rug wool 4
1 bamboo 3
1 rug wool 4
3 jute 1, 2, 1
1 multiple yarns 4
Repeat ×18
8 jute 1, 2 ×4
1 carpet warp 3
1 chenille 4
1 carpet warp 3
8 jute 2, 1 ×4

TABLE LOOMS:
For pedal 1 use levers 1 + 2
For pedal 2 use levers 3 + 4
For pedal 3 use lever 2
For pedal 4 use lever 4

REQUIREMENTS: 3½ yd. warp
Linen, 1 lb. 13 oz.
Jute, 2 lbs.
Bamboo, 18 strips
Rug wool, 4 oz.
Carpet warp, ½ oz.
Multiple yarns, 50 yds. each single length
Chenille, 19 pieces 84" long. Secure ends together and twist until as long as rug is wide. Insert in the shed and beat hard.

WARP: Natural 10/3 linen @ 1000 yds. per lb.

WEFT:
Natural 2 ply jute @ 300 yds. per lb.
Natural rug wool @ 225 yds. per lb.
Beige wool chenille selvages
Natural heavy bamboo strips ³⁄₁₆" wide
Natural 8/4 carpet warp
Multiple yarns used together
    1 lt. olive rug wool
    2 natural rug wool
    2 lt. grey rug wool
    2 jute & viscose @ 1200 yds. per lb.
    1 natural heavy rug wool

WARP ENDS: 504

ENDS PER INCH: 12

REED: 12

WIDTH IN REED: 42"

DENTING: 1 per dent

THREAD: Single in heddle 1, 2, 3, 4

PLACE MATS

Standard place mat sizes are 12″ × 18″ and 14″ × 20″; however, with various size tables and the popular breakfast counter, mat sizes will be adjusted to individual requirements.

Mats may be woven either warp length or weft length.

To weave warp length mats, the width of the warp will determine the depth of the mat as it is used on the table. Selvages will be across the top of the mat and at the bottom, at the table's edge. The length of the mat as it is used on the table will be determined by the amount woven. Extra must be woven for hems at the start and end of each mat, or in the case of fringe, warp allowance for fringe must be made between mats. Strips of 1″ wide, not too heavy paper are inserted in alternate sheds, and weaving continues. The number of strips is determined by the number of inches of warp required. For tied fringe, at least 3″ should be left at the end of each mat, and another 3″ for the end of the next mat, making a total of 6″ warp allowance between mats.

Other methods of finishing, such as hemstitching, overcasting, cross stitching, and blanket stitching, require only one inch warp allowance at the end of each mat, making two inches to be left between mats. Mats with fringe may also be machine stitched. Weave a few shots beyond the end of the mat. When removed from the loom "pull" a weft thread. Machine stitch on this in matching thread, but do not machine fasten the ends. Leave ends with enough to hand-tie to fasten, then with a needle weave the ends back into the mat. Ravel weft to form fringe.

To weave weft length mats, the warp width becomes the length of the mat. Selvages occur at the sides of the mat, and hems will be at the top and at the bottom, parallel to the table's edge. These mats do not have fringe, and may be woven "by the yard," allowing enough weaving for desired depth of each mat plus hems. An example of this type of place mat is shown on page 96.

There is a preference today for the heavier mat, especially for informal settings. In any case, the mat should have a firm character, achieved by the use of rather heavy wefts, plied cottons, or at least partial use of linen as weft, or as an all linen warp with cotton weft. Mixed cotton and linen warps should be avoided because of tension problems. Choice of yarn colors should be made with consideration for the china to be used with them.

All mats must have one essential requirement, which is the ability to lie flat on the table with no protruding clumps to upset the goblets or cause the plates to be unsteady. Keep all heavy wefts uniformly flat.

When the character of the mat is not suitable for napkins, weave them in solid color linen yarn in plain weave.

In all linen mats, expect one inch shrinkage in width, and up to 1½″ in length per mat. Cotton mats will draw in to 2″ in width, with 2 to 3″ take-up per mat.

The table stole is also popular, and is included here as many mats may be extended to stole length. One stole or two are used together, either placed directly on the table, or Scandinavian style, as an accent over a white linen cloth. They are especially nice for the buffet supper table.

PLACE MATS

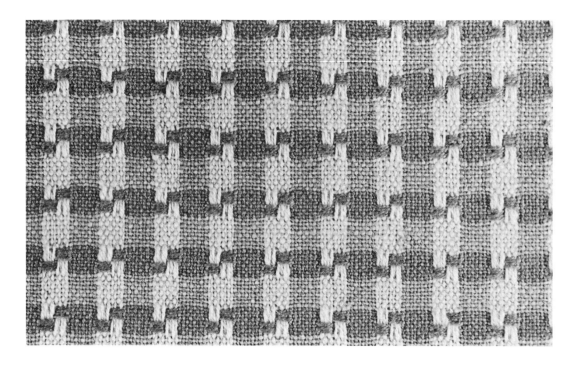

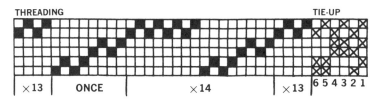

THREADING   TIE-UP

×13   ONCE   ×14   ×13 6 5 4 3 2 1

WARP: Swedish 22/2 cottolin, 54% cotton, 46% linen @ 3250 yds. per lb.
   Natural
   Mustard
WEFT: Same as warp
WARP ENDS: 336
ENDS PER INCH: 24
REED: 12
WIDTH IN REED: 14″
DENTING: 2 per dent
THREAD: Single in heddle
Mustard 6, 5 ×26
Natural 4, 3, 4, 3⎫
Natural 2, 1, 2, 1⎬×14
Mustard 6, 5 ×4 ⎭
Natural 4, 3, 4, 3
Natural 2, 1, 2, 1
Mustard 6, 5 ×26

WARPING ORDER:
52 mustard
   8 natural ⎫
   8 mustard ⎬×14
   8 natural
52 mustard
TREADLING:
3″ mustard 1, 2 (1″ for hem + 2″)
Mustard 3, 4, 3, 4, 5, 6, 5, 6⎫
Natural 1, 2 ×4   ⎬×22
Mustard 3, 4, 3, 4, 5, 6, 5, 6
3″ mustard 1, 2
REQUIREMENTS: For 6 mats 13″ × 18″
A 5 yd. warp includes loom allowance
Total amounts for warp and weft
      Natural 6 oz.
      Mustard 10 oz.

(94)

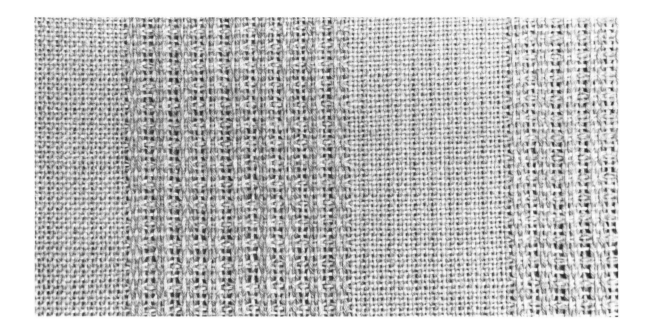

4 harness, 3 pedal

LACE WEAVE

WARP: Unmercerized 4 ply cotton @ 2700
yds. or 12/4 @ 2520 yds. per lb.
      Emerald
      Peacock

WEFT: Green 20/1 linen @ 6000 yds. per
lb.—doubled

WARP ENDS: 282

ENDS PER INCH: 20

REED: 10

WIDTH IN REED: 14″ + 1 dent

DENTING: 2 per dent

THREAD: Single in heddle
Block **A** 3, 4, 1, 4, 1, 4
Block **B** 3, 4, 2, 4, 2, 4
A ×5
B ×3
A ×5
B ×6
A ×9
B ×6
A ×5
B ×3
A ×5
Thread at random, emerald or peacock

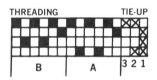

WARPING ORDER:
1 emerald
1 peacock
Warp the two ends together, 141 ends of
    each.

TREADLING: Doubled weft
18″ 1, 2, 1, 2, 1, 3
Allow for fringes or weave for hems and
    continue weaving for second mat.

TABLE LOOMS:
For pedal 1 use levers 1 + 2 + 3
For pedal 2 use levers 1 + 4
For pedal 3 use lever 4

REQUIREMENTS: For one mat including
    fringe or hems
Warp: Emerald 94 yds.
        Peacock 94 yds.
Weft: 300 yds.

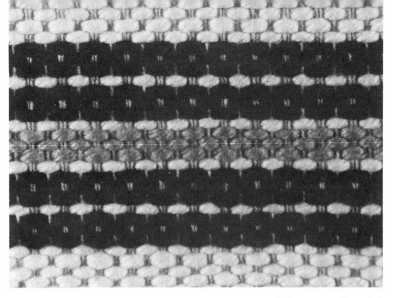

2 harness, 2 pedal

WARP: Beige 8/4 carpet warp

WEFT: Rug weave yarn, rayon and cotton @ 70 yds. per skein
Ivory
Black
Cerise

THREADING   TIE-UP
2 1

WARP ENDS: 105

ENDS PER INCH: 7½

REED: 10

WIDTH IN REED: 14″

DENTING:
1 per dent
1 empty dent
2 per dent
1 empty dent

THREAD: Single in heddle
1
2 ×2

TREADLING:
8 ivory 1, 2 ×4
3 black 1, 2, 1 } ×2
1 ivory 2 }
3 cerise 1, 2, 1
1 ivory 2
3 black 1, 2, 1 } ×2
1 ivory 2 }
15″ ivory 1, 2
Leave 1½″ black and cerise extended at selvages. Trim to 1″.

REQUIREMENTS: For 6 mats 12″ × 18″
A 5 yd. warp includes loom allowance
Warp: 5 oz.
Weft: Ivory, 4 skeins
Black 28 yds.
Cerise 7 yds.

PLACE MAT 4 harness, 2 pedal

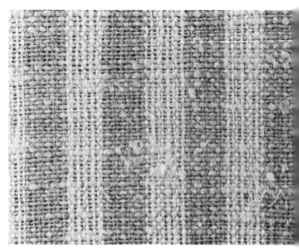

PLAIN WEAVE

WARP: Swedish 22/2 cottolin @ 3250 yds. per lb.
Natural
Mustard

THREADING   TIE-UP
2 1

WEFT: Natural slub linen

WARP ENDS: 342

ENDS PER INCH: 18

REED: 12

WIDTH IN REED: 19″

DENTING:
1 per dent
2 per dent
Repeat

THREAD: Single in heddle
Follow warping order 1, 2, 3, 4

WARPING ORDER:
55 mustard
8 natural }
8 mustard } ×14
8 natural
55 mustard

TREADLING: 1, 2
14″ per mat includes hems

TABLE LOOMS:
Levers: 1 + 3
2 + 4

REQUIREMENTS: For 6 mats 18″ × 12″
A 4 yd. warp includes loom allowance
Warp: Mustard 4 oz.
Natural 3 oz.
Weft: 8 oz.

PLACE MAT

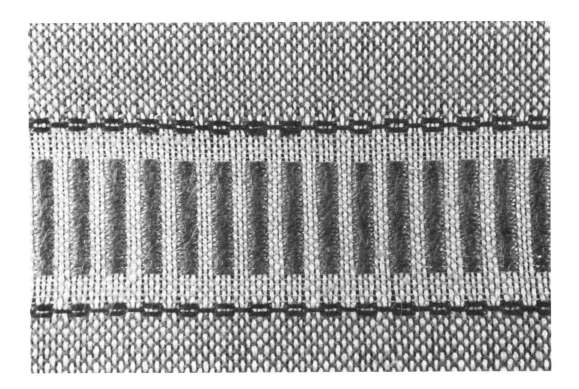

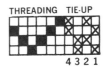

THREADING TIE-UP

4 3 2 1

WARP: 16/2 or 14/2 natural linen

WEFT: 10/2 linen
   Tan
   Lt. brown
   Brown
   16/1 natural linen

WARP ENDS: 196

ENDS PER INCH: 15

REED: 15

WIDTH IN REED: 13″ + 1 dent

DENTING: 1 per dent

THREAD: Single in heddle 4, 3, 2, 1, 2, 3

REQUIREMENTS: 5 yd. warp for 6 mats
   includes loom allowance

Warp: ½ lb.

Weft: Tan ½ lb.
   Lt. brown 2 oz.
   Brown ½ oz.
   16/1 natural 2 oz.

May be woven on the same warp as page
   103.

TREADLING:

1½″ tan 1, 2

Pattern stripe

$\begin{cases} \text{3 brown 3, 4, 3} \\ \text{6 natural 1, 2} \times 3 \\ \text{1 lt. brown 3} \\ \text{1 natural 1} \\ \text{1 lt. brown 3} \\ \text{1 natural 2} \\ \text{1 lt. brown} \\ \text{6 natural 1, 2} \times 3 \\ \text{3 brown 3, 4, 3} \end{cases}$

Middle bracket group $\times 13$

12″ tan 1, 2

Repeat pattern stripe

1½″ tan

TABLE LOOMS:

For pedal 1 use levers 1 + 3
For pedal 2 use levers 2 + 4
For pedal 3 use levers 1 + 2
For pedal 4 use levers 3 + 4

PLACE MAT 4 harness, 6 pedal   TABLE STOLE

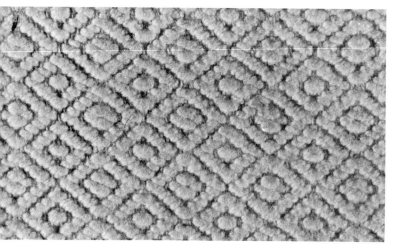

THREADING   TIE-UP

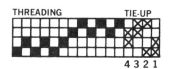

6 5 4 3 2 1

TABLE LOOMS:
For pedal 1 use levers 2 + 4
For pedal 2 use levers 1 + 3
For pedal 3 use levers 3 + 4
For pedal 4 use levers 2 + 3
For pedal 5 use levers 1 + 2
For pedal 6 use levers 1 + 4

REQUIREMENTS: 5 yd. warp for 6 mats
Warp: 10 oz.

Weft: 12 skeins

WARP: Natural 10/2 ramie @ 1500 yds.
  per lb.

WEFT: Natural rayon-cotton rug weave @
  70 yds. per skein

WARP ENDS: 168

ENDS PER INCH: 12

REED: 12

WIDTH IN REED: 14″

DENTING: 1 per dent

THREAD: Single in heddle
4, 3, 2, 1 ×2
2, 3, 4
1, 2, 3

TREADLING: Ramie heading 1, 2, 1, 2
3, 4, 5, 6 ×2
5, 4, 3
6, 5, 4
Weave 20″
Ramie 1, 2, 1, 2

TABLE STOLE

4 harness, 4 pedal

THREADING   TIE-UP

4 3 2 1

WARP: Natural 10/2 unmercerized cotton
  @ 4200 yds. per lb.

WEFT: Biscuit 10/2 linen @ 1500 yds.
  per lb.

WARP ENDS: 360

ENDS PER INCH: 24

REED: 12

WIDTH IN REED: 15″

DENTING: 2 per dent

THREAD: Single in heddle
4, 3 ×3
2, 1 ×3

TREADLING: 1, 2, 3, 4, 3, 2, 1, 4
TABLE LOOMS:
Levers: 1 + 2
1 + 4
3 + 4
2 + 3
3 + 4
1 + 4
1 + 2
2 + 3

REQUIREMENTS: For a 4 yd. warp
Warp: 6 oz.
Weft: 10 oz. for 3 yds.

DOUBLE WIDTH CLOTH 68" x 102" 4 harness, 4 pedal

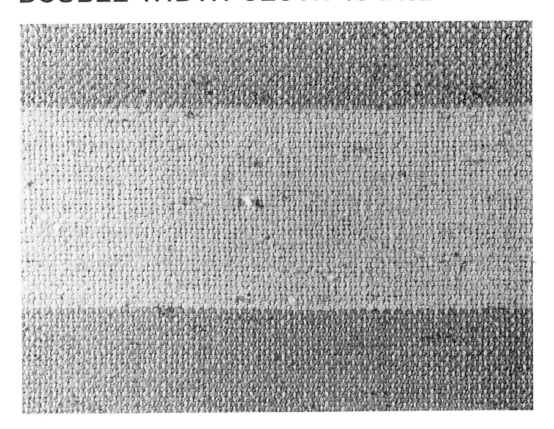

THREADING TIE-UP

4 3 2 1

WARP: Natural swedish 22/2 cottolin @ 3250 yds. per lb.

WEFT: Natural cottolin
Natural rayon flake @ } Wound together
4500 yds.
Yellow cottolin } Wound together
Chartreuse rayon flake

WARP ENDS: 1052

ENDS PER INCH: 30

REED: 15

WIDTH IN REED: 35" + 2 dents

Important: After threading remove the first end on harness 1 and discard, then proceed with denting from the right

DENTING:
1 per dent
1 empty dent
2 per dent for remainder

THREAD: Single in heddle 1, 2, 3, 4

TREADLING: To begin: Throw shuttle from the right

Tread 1, 2, 3, 4
2" natural } ×26
2" yellow
2" natural

TABLE LOOMS:
For pedal 1 use levers 1 + 2 + 3
For pedal 2 use levers 1 + 3 + 4
For pedal 3 use lever 1
For pedal 4 use lever 3

REQUIREMENTS: 4 yd. warp
Natural cottolin, 2 lbs.
Yellow cottolin, 1 lb.
Natural flake, 1 lb.
Chartreuse flake, 1 lb.

PLACE MAT

WARP: Natural 10/2 ramie @ 1500 yds. per lb.

WEFT: Pink 2 ply jute @ 300 yds. per lb.
White spun rayon @ 1200 yds. per lb.
Lt. green 10/2 linen @ 1500 yds. per lb.

WARP ENDS: 168

ENDS PER INCH: 12

REED: 12

WIDTH IN REED: 14″

DENTING: 1 per dent

THREAD: Single in heddle
4, 3, 2, 1 ×2
2, 3, 4, 1, 2, 3

REQUIREMENTS: 5 yd. warp for 6 mats 12″ × 18″
Warp: 10 oz.
Weft: Pink, 1 lb.
White 4 oz.
Green 1 oz.

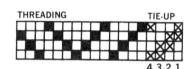

THREADING   TIE-UP
4 3 2 1

TREADLING:
Heading: 4 white 4, 3, 2, 1
7 pink 4, 3, 2, 1, 2, 3, 4 ⎫
4 white 1, 2, 3, 4   ⎬ ×17
1 green 1   ⎪
4 white 4, 3, 2, 1   ⎭
7 pink 4, 3, 2, 1, 2, 3, 4
4 white 1, 2, 3, 4
Allow for fringes or hems between mats

TABLE LOOMS:
For pedal 1 use levers 3 + 4
For pedal 2 use levers 2 + 3
For pedal 3 use levers 1 + 2
For pedal 4 use levers 1 + 4

PLACE MAT

LACE WEAVE

WARP: White 20/2 linen @ 3000 yds. per lb.

      Shell pink 10/2 linen @ 1500 yds.

WEFT: Copper and silver twist shell pink 10/2 merc. cotton

WARP ENDS: 283

ENDS PER INCH: 20

REED: 10

WIDTH IN REED: 14″ + 1 dent

DENTING: 2 per dent except 3 in last dent

THREAD: Single in heddle

Follow warping order

Block **A** 3, 4, 1, 4, 1, 4

Block **B** 3, 4, 2, 4, 2, 4

C 3

A ×5
B ×3
A ×5
B ×6
A ×9
B ×6
A ×5
B ×3
A ×5
C ×1

TREADLING: 18″

1, 2, 1, 2, 1, 3

TABLE LOOMS:

For pedal 1 use levers 1 + 2 + 3

For pedal 2 use levers 1 + 4

For pedal 3 use lever 4

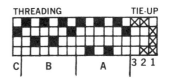

WARPING ORDER:

1 white }×5
5 pink

18 white

1 white }×5
5 pink

36 white

1 white }×9
5 pink

36 white

1 white }×5
5 pink

18 white

1 white }×5
5 pink

1 white

REQUIREMENTS: For one mat including fringe

Warp: White, 92 yds.

     Pink, 94 yds.

Weft: 150 yds.

Use two warp beams or cut and re-tie between mats.

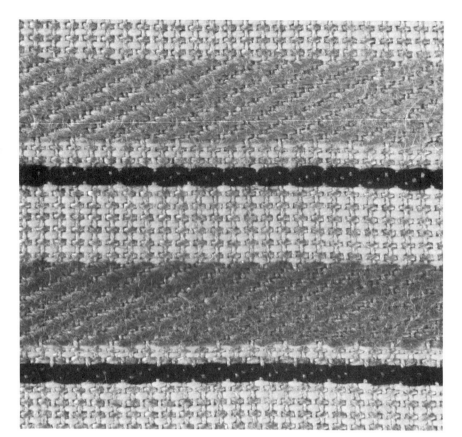

TABLE STOLE

14" x 90"

4 harness, 6 pedal

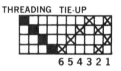

THREADING TIE-UP

6 5 4 3 2 1

WARP: Natural 14/2 linen @ 2100 yds.

WEFT: Natural heavy 4/4 carpet warp
@ 800 yds. per lb.
Natural jute and rayon twist
@ 1200 yds.
Single ply jute @ 1200 yds. per lb.
Lime   Med. blue
Coral   Dk. brown

WARP ENDS: 152

ENDS PER INCH: 10

REED: 10

WIDTH IN REED: 15" + 2 dents

DENTING: 1 per dent

THREAD: Single in heddle 1, 2, 3, 4

REQUIREMENTS: 4 yd. warp, 6 oz.
Weft:
Jute and rayon, 5 oz.
Carpet warp ½ lb.
Single ply jute 1 oz. each color

TREADLING: Weave 1" for hem 1, 2

A $\begin{bmatrix} 1 \text{ carpet warp } 1 \\ 1 \text{ jute \& rayon } 2 \end{bmatrix} \times 10$
    4 brown 3, 4, 5, 6
    A ×2
    12 blue 3, 4, 5, 6 ×3
    6 coral 3, 4, 5, 6, 3, 4
    A ×6
    4 brown 3, 4, 5, 6
    A ×2
    18 lime 3, 4, 5, 6 ×4 + 3, 4
    A ×7
    4 brown 3, 4, 5, 6
    A ×16
    4 coral 3, 4, 5, 6 } ×2
    A ×7
    4 coral—repeat in reverse
    Repeat the whole 4 more times
    1" for hem 1, 2

TABLE LOOMS:
For pedal 1 use levers 2 + 4
For pedal 2 use levers 1 + 3
For pedal 3 use lever 4
For pedal 4 use lever 3
For pedal 5 use lever 2
For pedal 6 use lever 1

TABLE STOLE

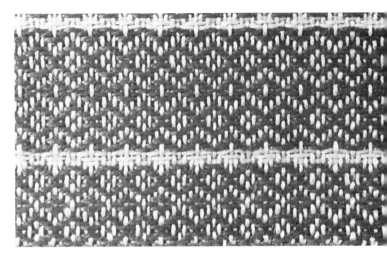

4 harness, 4 pedal

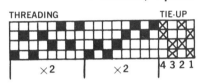

M'S AND O'S

WARP: Natural soft twist 8/2 cotton @ 3360 yds. per lb.

WEFT: Lime single ply jute @ 1200 yds. per lb.

WARP ENDS: 336

ENDS PER INCH: 24

REED: 12

WIDTH IN REED: 14″

DENTING: 2 per dent

THREAD: Single in heddle

$$\left.\begin{array}{l}4, 3 \times 2 \\ 2, 1 \times 2\end{array}\right\} \times 2$$
$$\left.\begin{array}{l}4, 2 \times 2 \\ 3, 1 \times 2\end{array}\right\} \times 2$$

TREADLING:
1, 2 ×3
3, 4 ×3

TABLE LOOMS:
Levers: $\left.\begin{array}{l}1 + 3 \\ 2 + 4\end{array}\right\} \times 3$
$\left.\begin{array}{l}1 + 2 \\ 3 + 4\end{array}\right\} \times 3$

REQUIREMENTS: 4 yd. warp, 7 oz.
Weft for 3 yards, ½ lb.

PLACE MAT

4 harness, 4 pedal

WARP: 16/2 or 14/2 natural linen

WEFT: 10/2 linen
Natural
Red

WARP ENDS: 196

ENDS PER INCH: 15

REED: 15

WIDTH IN REED: 13″ + 1 dent

DENTING: 1 per dent

THREAD: Single in heddle 4, 3, 2, 1, 2, 3

TREADLING:
1, 2, 3, 4, 3, 2, 1,
4, 3, 2, 1, 2, 3, 4
21 red
 3 natural
29 red
 3 natural
Red for 13″ (center)
Repeat border in reverse

TABLE LOOMS:
For pedal 1 use levers 1 + 2
For pedal 2 use levers 2 + 3
For pedal 3 use levers 3 + 4
For pedal 4 use levers 1 + 4

REQUIREMENTS: 5 yd. warp for 6 mats
  includes loom allowance
Warp: ½ lb.
Weft: Red, 10 oz.
    Natural ½ oz.
May be woven on the same warp as page 97.

PLACE MAT

MONK'S BELT

WARP: Natural 10/2 cotton @ 4200 yds.
 per lb.

WEFT: Tabby same as warp
  Pearl 3
    Black
    Gold

WARP ENDS: 318

ENDS PER INCH: 24

REED: 12

WIDTH IN REED: 13″ + 3 dents

DENTING: 2 per dent

THREAD: Single in heddle

4, 3 ×3 }
2, 1 ×3 } ×26

4, 3 ×3

REQUIREMENTS: 5 yd. warp for 6 mats
Warp and weft 10/2 cotton, 10 oz.
Black pearl, 4 oz.
Gold pearl, 1 oz.

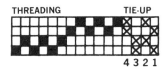

THREADING   TIE-UP

4 3 2 1

TREADLING: One tabby shot 1, 2 between
 every pattern shot 3, 4
2″ ground 1, 2 (includes hem)
27 black 3
12 gold 4 ×4
    3 ×4
    4 ×4
27 black 3
12″ ground 1, 2
Repeat pattern
2″ ground

TABLE LOOMS:
For pedal 1 use levers 1 + 3
For pedal 2 use levers 2 + 4
For pedal 3 use levers 1 + 2
For pedal 4 use levers 3 + 4

FASHION FABRICS

There is something very gratifying about weaving a length of wool, and either wearing or seeing some member of the family wearing a garment made from it.

Weaving wool isn't any more difficult than any other type of weaving, although there seems to be a notion it is. Since it has great elasticity, a wool warp will tension adjust to a much greater extent than linen and some hard twisted cottons. The weft must not be beaten too hard, otherwise a harsh, stiff fabric will result after finishing. Selvages should be neat, as a matter of pride, care must be taken in the finishing, but with these mastered, the weaving of wool brings great satisfaction, and a fabric which will far outwear any power-loomed piece. This result is achieved not only by the weaver, but by the yarns used. The power loom cannot handle all the lovely soft yarns the handweaver is allowed. Breakage at such a high speed as power weaving occurs too often with yarns especially spun for the handweaver.

The garment that is wanted will determine the type of yarn to use. After that, color, pattern, and set will be considered.

There is some confusion about the difference between wool and worsted yarns. They are both "wool", as we know it, the difference is in the carding and combing of the yarn. Wool yarn is carded, but not combed. It is typically a single ply yarn, with much of the animal oil known as lanolin left in the yarn to add strength during weaving. This then must be washed (scoured) out after the length has been removed from the loom. The oil tends to dull the colors to quite an extent, and for this reason samples should be made and scoured exactly as the finished piece is to be before final selection of yarn colors, and their effect on one another. This is the yarn used in tweeds usually associated with coats and men's wear fabrics. Some yarns give a soft, light fabric, and some a hairy, almost harsh surface. Both are desirable, depending on what is wanted. Most tweed yarns are designed to be used as both warp and weft. Some manufacturers twist the warp a bit tighter than the weft, and indicate which should be used for warp or weft.

The size or thickness of the yarn is indicated by the "cut" There are 300 yards in 1 cut wool, 3000 in 10 cut, and so on. A 6 cut yarn set at 15 ends per inch will produce a heavy twill fabric. For a still heavy, but lighter weight tweed, use a 9 cut set at 20, and for a 12 cut, a set of 24 will produce a lighter weight, but heavy enough fabric for suits, jackets, and topcoats. For a lightweight wool shirting or dress fabric, set 16 cut at 30 ends per inch.

Wool should be sleyed at 2 per dent, even if it leaves skipped dents. A set of 15 ends per inch in a 15 reed should be 2 per dent, one empty dent, etc., to avoid friction in shed changing.

Great shrinkage occurs in wool. Warp width will shrink to 4", and length to 8", and even 10" per yard after finishing.

This then is a warning in calculating warp lengths.

There are probably as many ways to finish tweed as there are weavers of it. Here is one tried and proved method. Wash by hand, never in a machine. Soak in luke-warm water with a few drops of ammonia for an hour. Wash in warm water with a mixture of soap flakes and detergent, half as much detergent as soap. Rinse, wash again; rinse 2 or 3 times. Gently squeeze, and towel-dry to extract water; roll on a large, blanket-covered paper tube for 24 hours. If possible, have another such blanketed roller; if not, the same should be given a dry cover, and used again. Re-roll the web on this with the dry outside end toward the roller, and the damp end on the outside. Leave for another 24 hours; repeat until fabric is dry. Pressing will not be necessary.

Tweeds are traditionally woven in twill, or some variation of twill, such as herringbone, broken twill, seed and crossed twill.

Tweeds are often mistakenly called "homespuns." Homespun is also woven of single ply wool yarn, the difference being that it is always woven in plain weave. Tabby, being a tighter weave than twill with less finishing shrinkage, allows for a closer set. A set of 18 ends with 18 picks is usual.

Worsted yarn differs from woolen yarn in that after carding, the fibers are combed until all the shorter ends are combed out, leaving only the longer fibers all lying in one direction. Worsted then may be spun very fine, a size 1 containing 560 yards per pound. Worsted is twisted into plied yarns, the size range mostly used by handweavers being 15/2 with 4200 yds. per lb., through sizes to 32/2 with 8960 yds. per lb.

The beginner in wool weaving will do well to choose worsted for both warp and weft. Being a plied yarn, it is much the easier to warp, beam, and weave. Also it contains no oil, and requires little or no finishing. The web should be steamed for shrinkage by a local dry cleaner or tailor, but specify steamed, not pressed. Worsted makes excellent dress fabric, suitings, lightweight coating, and scarfs.

Men's wear is usually turned over to a competent tailor, but the home sewer will find it rewarding to cut and sew her own fabric. The selection of a pattern should be made before weaving. Even 20" looms will weave fabric wide enough for many patterns. The widest pattern piece will determine how wide the warp must be set plus 4" allowance. All pattern pieces are then placed so that this width is not exceeded. Pieces will be adjusted and re-adjusted, always keeping the straight line indicated on the pattern. Since the warp width has already been established, the finished length will be found by the total length of all the pieces. To this add take-up, finishing shrinkage, and loom waste allowances. From this the warp yarn is estimated. Weft will take only slightly less yarn than the warp.

For safety, always order a little more than is indicated. Leftover yarn can always be woven into scarfs, pillows, and other small weavings.

4 harness, 4 pedal

TWILL

WARP: 20/2 worsted @ 5600 yds. per lb.
  Lt. blue
  Med. blue
  Lt. green
  Med. green

WEFT: Same as warp

WARP ENDS: 864

ENDS PER INCH: 24

REED: 12

WIDTH IN REED: 36″

DENTING: 2 per dent

THREAD: Single in heddle 1, 2, 3, 4
Follow warping order

WARPING ORDER:
28 med. green
10 lt. green
10 med. blue
20 lt. blue
10 med. blue
10 lt. green

THREADING TIE-UP

4 3 2 1

TREADLING: 1, 2, 3, 4
28 med. blue
10 med. green
10 lt. green
20 lt. blue
10 lt. green
10 med. green

TABLE LOOMS:
For pedal 1 use levers 3 + 4
For pedal 2 use levers 2 + 3
For pedal 3 use levers 1 + 2
For pedal 4 use levers 1 + 4

REQUIREMENTS: For 1 yd.
1¾ oz. of each color

WORSTED

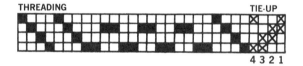

THREADING   TIE-UP

4 3 2 1

WARP: 20/2 worsted @ 5600 yds. per lb.
         Black
         Olive
WEFT: Black 20/2 worsted
WARP ENDS: 900
ENDS PER INCH: 25
REED: 12
WIDTH IN REED: 36″
DENTING:
2 per dent for 8 dents
3 per dent once
2 per dent for 3 dents
THREAD: single in heddle
4 olive 1, 2, 3, 4
2 black 1 ×2
2 olive 3 ×2 ⎤
2 olive 1 ×2 ⎦ ×2
2 olive 3 ×2
2 black 1 ×2
7 olive 2, 3, 4, 1, 2, 3, 4

WARPING ORDER:
  4 olive ⎤
  2 black ⎥
10 olive ⎬ ×36
  2 black ⎥
  7 olive ⎦
TREADLING: 1, 2, 3, 4
TABLE LOOMS:
Levers: 3 + 4
        2 + 3
        1 + 2
        1 + 4
REQUIREMENTS: For 1 yd.
Approx. 7 oz. worsted
           4 oz. black
           3 oz. olive

WORSTED AND MOHAIR LOOP   4 harness, 4 pedal

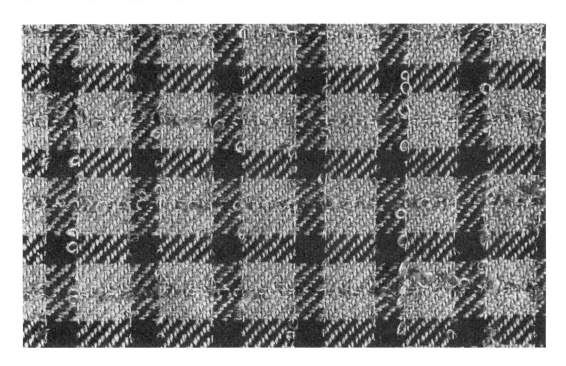

THREADING   TIE-UP

4 3 2 1

TWILL

WARP: 20/2 worsted @ 5600 yds. per lb.
   Emerald
   Peacock
   Dark blue
  Mohair loop @ 2400 yds. per lb.
   Emerald
   Peacock

WEFT: Same as warp

WARP ENDS: 864

ENDS PER INCH: 24

REED: 12

WIDTH IN REED: 36″

DENTING: 2 per dent

THREAD: Single in heddle 1, 2, 3, 4
Follow warping order

WARPING ORDER:
8 dark blue
1 peacock mohair
7 peacock worsted
7 emerald worsted
1 emerald mohair

TREADLING:
8 dark blue 1, 2, 3, 4 ×2
7 peacock worsted 1, 2, 3, 4, 1, 2, 3
1 peacock mohair 4
1 emerald mohair 1
7 emerald worsted 2, 3, 4, 1, 2, 3, 4

TABLE LOOMS:
For pedal 1 use levers 3 + 4
For pedal 2 use levers 2 + 3
For pedal 3 use levers 1 + 2
For pedal 4 use levers 1 + 4

REQUIREMENTS: For 1 yd.
Worsted:
  Dark blue 2 oz.
  Peacock 2 oz.
  Emerald 2 oz.
Mohair:
  Peacock ¾ oz.
  Emerald ¾ oz.

WORSTED   8 harness, 8 pedal   4 harness, 2 pedal

THREADING   TIE-UP

87654321

WORSTED WEAVE

WARP: 20/2 worsted @ 5600 yds. per lb.
Dk. orange
Chestnut
WEFT: Same as warp
WARP ENDS: 864
ENDS PER INCH: 24
REED: 12
WIDTH IN REED: 36″
DENTING: 2 per dent
THREAD: Single in heddle
1, 2 orange
3, 4, 5, 6 chestnut
7, 8 orange

WARPING ORDER:
2 orange
4 chestnut
2 orange

TREADLING:
1, 2 orange
3, 4, 5, 6 chestnut
7, 8 orange

REQUIREMENTS: For 1 yd.
Dk. orange 3½ oz.
Chestnut 3½ oz.

PLAIN WEAVE

WARP: 20/2 worsted @ 5600 yds. per lb.
Dark green
Mustard

THREADING   TIE-UP

2 1

WEFT: Same as warp
WARP ENDS: 864
ENDS PER INCH: 24
REED: 12
WIDTH IN REED: 36″
DENTING: 2 per dent
THREAD: Single in heddle
Green 1, 2, 3, 4 ×2
Mustard 1, 2, 3, 4 ×2
WARPING ORDER:
8 green
8 mustard

TREADLING: 1, 2
8 green
8 mustard
TABLE LOOMS:
Levers: 1 + 3
2 + 4
REQUIREMENTS: For 1 yd.
Green 3 oz.
Mustard 3 oz.
20/2 worsted set at 24 in plain weave pro-
duces a tight, rather stiff fabric suitable
for sun-shower wear.

NOVELTY WEAVE

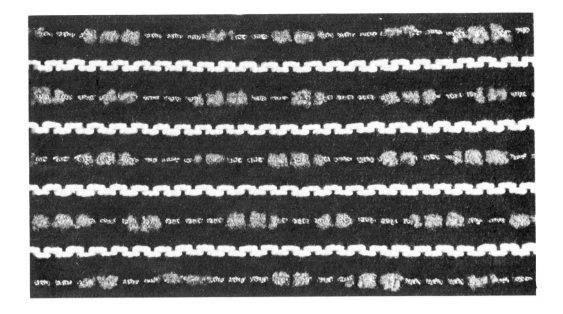

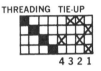

4 3 2 1

WARP: Black 20/2 worsted @ 5600 yds.
 per lb.

WEFT: Black rayon flake @ 4500 yds.
 per lb., doubled
 Natural 5/2 rayon or merc.
 cotton @ 2100 yds. per lb.
 Copper rayon novelty yarn

WARP ENDS: 864

ENDS PER INCH: 24

REED: 12

WIDTH IN REED: 36"

DENTING: 2 per dent

THREAD: Single in heddle 1, 2, 3, 4

TREADLING:
5 doubled black 1, 2, 1, 2, 1
2 natural 3, 4
5 doubled black 1, 2, 1, 2, 1
1 copper 3

TABLE LOOMS:
For pedal 1 use levers 1 + 3
For pedal 2 use levers 2 + 4
For pedal 3 use lever 4
For pedal 4 use lever 2

REQUIREMENTS: For 1 yd.
Warp, 3 oz.
Black flake, 5 oz.
Natural, 150 yds.
Copper, 75 yds.
May be woven on the same warp as on
 pages 119, 120.

(111)

TWEEDS

1

2

WARP: Brown heather 12 cut wool in oil @ 3600 yds. per lb.

WEFT: No. 1. Taffy heather 12 cut wool
No. 2. Same as warp

WARP ENDS: 792

ENDS PER INCH: 24

REED: 12

WIDTH IN REED: 33"

DENTING: 2 per dent

THREAD: Single in heddle 1, 2, 3, 4

TREADLING: 1, 2, 3, 4

THREADING TIE-UP
4 3 2 1

TABLE LOOMS:
For pedal 1 use levers 3 + 4
For pedal 2 use levers 2 + 3
For pedal 3 use levers 1 + 2
For pedal 4 use levers 1 + 4

REQUIREMENTS: For 1 yd.
No. 1. Brown heather 4 oz.
Taffy heather 4 oz.
No. 2. Brown heather 8 oz.
Tweed must be scoured. 33" will finish to approx. 30". An 8 yard warp will finish to approx. 6¼ yds.

WARP: Lt. tan 17/2 worsted @ 4760 yds. per lb.

WEFT: Flecked tan wool @ 2000 yds. per lb.

WARP ENDS: 660

ENDS PER INCH: 20

REED: 10

WIDTH IN REED: 33"

DENTING: 2 per dent

THREAD: Single in heddle 1, 2, 3, 4

TREADLING: 1, 2, 3, 4

REQUIREMENTS: For 1 yd.
Worsted 3 oz.
Wool 6 oz.

THREADING TIE-UP
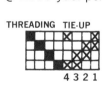
4 3 2 1

WORSTED

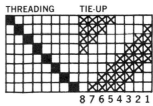

THREADING   TIE-UP

8 7 6 5 4 3 2 1

4/4 TWILL

WARP: 20/2 worsted @ 5600 yds. per lb.
        Black
        Natural
        Lt. brown

WEFT: Same as warp

WARP ENDS: 864

ENDS PER INCH: 24

REED: 12

WIDTH IN REED: 36″

DENTING: 2 per dent

THREAD: Single in heddle
1, 2, 3, 4, 5, 6, 7, 8
Follow warping order

WARPING ORDER:
16 lt. brown
 8 natural
 8 black
 8 natural   ×15
 8 black
 8 natural
16 lt. brown
 8 natural

TREADLING: 1, 2, 3, 4, 5, 6, 7, 8
Follow warping order

REQUIREMENTS: For 1 yd.
Black 2¼ oz.
Natural 2¼ oz.
Lt. brown 2½ oz.

4 harness,
4 pedal

2

1

HERRINGBONE VARIATION

WARP: Norwegian "Ullspissgarn"
  @ approx. 640 yds.
Skeins are approx. 175 yds. per skein
No. 1. Lt. red
No. 2. Grey
WEFT:
No. 1. Same as warp
No. 2. Dark brown heather "Ullspissgarn"
WARP ENDS: 420
ENDS PER INCH: 12
REED: 12
WIDTH IN REED: 35″
DENTING:
2 per dent
1 empty dent
Repeat

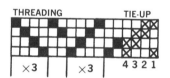

THREADING   TIE-UP
×3   ×3   4 3 2 1

THREAD: Single in heddle
2, 1
4, 3, 2, 1 ×3
3, 4
1, 2, 3, 4 ×3
TREADLING: 1, 2, 3, 4
TABLE LOOMS:
Levers: 1 + 4
        3 + 4
        2 + 3
        1 + 2
REQUIREMENTS: For 1 yd.
Warp and weft, 5 skeins
Heavy coating

THREADING | TIE-UP

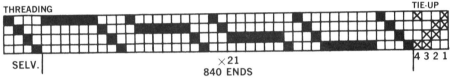

SELV. | ×21 840 ENDS | 4 3 2 1

DIAGONAL RIB WEAVE

WARP: Oatmeal 20/2 worsted @ 5600 yds. per lb.

WEFT: Black 20/2 worsted

WARP ENDS: 840 + 4 left selv. = 844

ENDS PER INCH: 24

REED: 12

WIDTH IN REED: 35″ + 2 dents

DENTING: 2 per dent

THREAD: 4 ends, 1 per heddle
6 ends, 2 per heddle

1, 2, 3, 4 ⎫
1 ×6 ⎪
2, 3, 4, 1 ⎪
2 ×6 ⎬ ×21
3, 4, 1, 2 ⎪
3 ×6 ⎪
4, 1, 2, 3 ⎪
4 ×6 ⎭
1, 2, 3, 4

TREADLING:

1, 2, 3, 4
1 ×6 shots
2, 3, 4, 1
2 ×6
3, 4, 1, 2
3 ×6
4, 1, 2, 3
4 ×6

For 6 shots of black, wind bobbin with doubled weft and throw 3 shots in the same shed.

TABLE LOOMS:

For pedal 1 use levers 3 + 4
For pedal 2 use levers 2 + 3
For pedal 3 use levers 1 + 2
For pedal 4 use levers 1 + 4

REQUIREMENTS: For 1 yd.
Warp 3 oz.
Weft 4 oz.

4 harness, 4 pedal

THREADING   TIE-UP

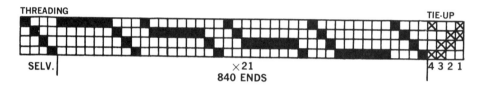

SELV.   ×21   4 3 2 1
840 ENDS

DIAGONAL RIB WEAVE

WARP: 20/2 worsted @ 5600 yds. per lb.
      Black
      White

WEFT: Black 20/2 worsted

WARP ENDS: 840 + 4 left selv. = 844

ENDS PER INCH: 24

REED: 12

WIDTH IN REED: 35″ + 2 dents

DENTING: 2 per dent

THREAD:

4 ends, 1 per heddle
6 ends, 2 per heddle

1, 2, 3, 4 ⎫
1 ×6   ⎪
2, 3, 4, 1 ⎪
2 ×6   ⎪
3, 4, 1, 2 ⎬ ×21
3 ×6   ⎪
4, 1, 2, 3 ⎪
4 ×6   ⎭
1, 2, 3, 4

WARPING ORDER:

4 black ⎫ ×84
6 white ⎭
4 selvage

TREADLING:

1, 2, 3, 4
1 ×6 shots
2, 3, 4, 1
2 ×6
3, 4, 1, 2
3 ×6
4, 1, 2, 3
4 ×6

For 6 shots of black, wind bobbin with doubled weft and throw 3 shots in the same shed.

TABLE LOOMS:

For pedal 1 use levers 3 + 4
For pedal 2 use levers 2 + 3
For pedal 3 use levers 1 + 2
For pedal 4 use levers 1 + 4

REQUIREMENTS: For 1 yd.
White 2 oz.
Black 5 oz.

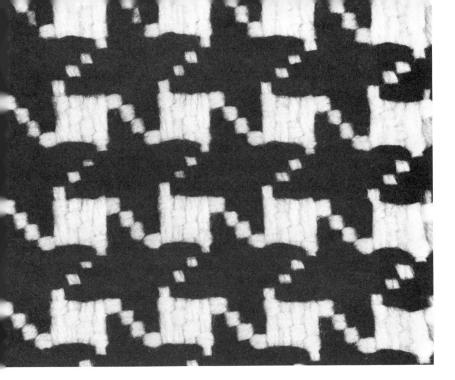

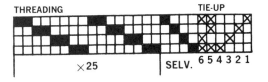

THREADING ... TIE-UP

×25 ... SELV. 6 5 4 3 2 1

HOUND'S TOOTH

WARP: 4 ply knitting worsted @ 980 yds.
  Black
  Off white

WEFT: Same as warp, doubled

WARP ENDS: 400 + 8 selv. = 408

ENDS PER INCH: 12

REED: 12

WIDTH IN REED: 34"

DENTING: Selvages 1 per dent
2 per dent
1 empty dent

THREAD: Selv. 1, 2, 3, 4

White $\begin{cases} 1 \times 2 \\ 2 \times 2 \\ 3 \times 2 \\ 4 \times 2 \end{cases}$

Black $\begin{cases} 1 \times 2 \\ 2 \times 2 \\ 3 \times 2 \\ 4 \times 2 \end{cases}$

REQUIREMENTS: For 1 yd.
White 8 oz.
Black 8 oz.
A lightweight, bulky, high-fashion coating

WARPING ORDER:
4 selv.
8 white
8 black $\Big\} \times 25$
4 selv.
Avoid stretching yarn.
Keep an even but fairly loose tension.

TREADLING: Doubled weft
Black 1, 2, 3, 4
White 1 + 2 + 3 together
  5
  6
  2 + 3 + 4

TABLE LOOMS:
Levers:
Black 4, 3, 2, 1
White 2 + 3 + 4
  1 + 3 + 4
  1 + 2 + 4
  1 + 2 + 3

TWEED

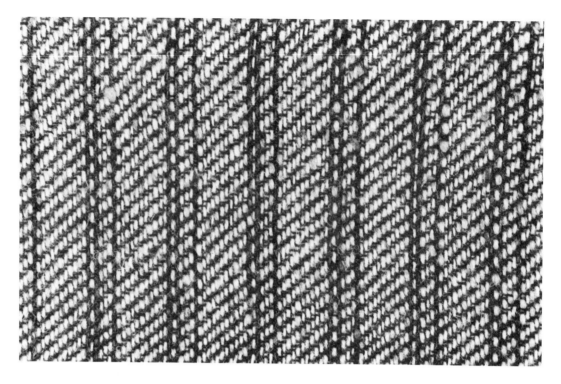

TWILL

WARP: Tweed wool @ 2720 yds. per lb.
Natural
Rust
Flecked beige tweed wool
Dark brown 12 cut wool

WEFT: Dark brown 12 cut wool @ 3600 yds. per lb.

WARP ENDS: 576

ENDS PER INCH: 18

REED: 9

WIDTH IN REED: 32"

DENTING: 2 per dent

THREAD: Single in heddle 1, 2, 3, 4
Follow warping order

REQUIREMENTS: For 1 yd.
Warp ¼ lb.
Weft ¼ lb.
Finish: Wash and press
A 6 yard warp will finish to approx. 4½ yds., enough for a man's jacket

THREADING   TIE-UP

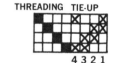

4 3 2 1

WARPING ORDER:
1 natural ⎫
1 beige ⎬ ×5
1 natural
1 brown
1 natural
1 beige
1 natural ⎫
1 rust   ⎬ ×2

TREADLING: 1, 2, 3, 4

TABLE LOOMS:
For pedal 1 use levers 3 + 4
For pedal 2 use levers 2 + 3
For pedal 3 use levers 1 + 2
For pedal 4 use levers 1 + 4

4 harness, 6 pedal

THREADING TIE-UP

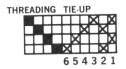

6 5 4 3 2 1

WARP: Black 20/2 worsted @ 5600 yds. per lb.

WEFT:

Rayon flake @ 4500 yds. per lb.

    Persian blue ⎫

    Emerald green ⎬ Wound together

    Dk. green ⎭

Pearl 3

    Black

    Natural

WARP ENDS: 864

ENDS PER INCH: 24

REED: 12

WIDTH IN REED: 36″

DENTING: 2 per dent

THREAD: Single in heddle 1, 2, 3, 4

TREADLING: 6″ repeat

2¾″ flake group 1, 2

  2 natural 3, 5

  4 flake 2, 1 ×2

  2 black 4, 6

  4 flake 1, 2 ×2

  2 black 3, 5

  2 natural 3, 5

  2 black 3, 5

  4 flake 2, 1 ×2

  2 natural 4, 3

  4 flake 2, 1 ×2

  2 black 4, 6

14 flake 1, 2 ×7

  2 black 3, 5

  2 natural 3, 5

  2 black 3, 5

  4 flake 2, 1 ×2

  2 natural 4, 6

  4 flake 1, 2 ×2

  1 black 3

  1 flake 2

  1 black 3

  3 flake 2, 1, 2

  6 natural 5, 4, 3, 4, 5, 6

TABLE LOOMS:
For pedal 1 use levers 2 + 4
For pedal 2 use levers 1 + 3
For pedal 3 use lever 4
For pedal 4 use lever 3
For pedal 5 use lever 2
For pedal 6 use lever 1

REQUIREMENTS: For 1 yd.
Warp, 3 oz.
Flake, 2 oz. of each color
Black, 100 yds.
Natural, 115 yds.

4 harness, 2 pedal

THREADING TIE-UP

2 1

WARP: Black 20/2 worsted @ 5600 yds. per lb.
WEFT: Dark brown "Woodpecker" @ 2720 yds. per lb.
WARP ENDS: 864
ENDS PER INCH: 24
REED: 12
WIDTH IN REED: 36"
DENTING: 2 per dent
THREAD: Single in heddle 1, 2, 3, 4

TREADLING: 1, 2
TABLE LOOMS:
Levers: 1 + 2
3 + 4
REQUIREMENTS: For 1 yd.
Black worsted, 3 oz.
Brown "Woodpecker" 3 oz.

May be woven on the same warp as on pages 113, 121.

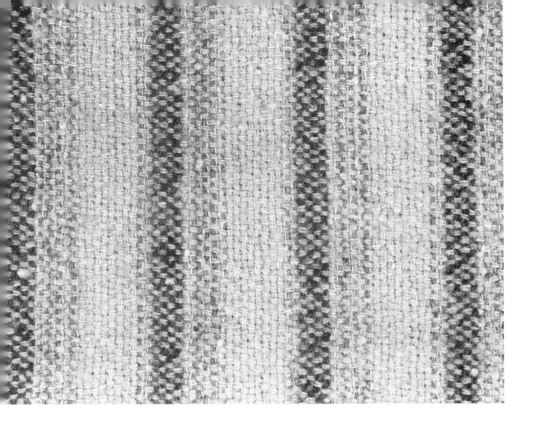

4 harness, 2 pedal

THREADING TIE-UP

2 1

WARP:
Single ply wool in oil @ 2200 yds.
> Lt. yellow
> Rose-grey heather
> Green
> Lt. tan

Rayon flake @ 4500 yds. per lb.
> Lime
> Lt. rose-grey
> Royal blue
> Emerald green
> Biscuit

WEFT:
1 lt. yellow wool same as warp } Wound
1 lime rayon same as warp } together

WARP ENDS: 600

ENDS PER INCH: 18

REED: 9

WIDTH IN REED: 33″ + 3 dents

DENTING: 2 per dent

THREAD: Doubled in heddle
(1 wool + 1 rayon)
1, 2, 3, 4

WARPING ORDER:
1 yellow wool } ×8
1 lime rayon }
1 grey wool } ×6
1 grey rayon }
1 green wool } ×3
1 royal rayon }
1 green wool
1 emerald rayon
1 lt. tan } ×2
1 biscuit }

TREADLING: Doubled weft 1, 2

TABLE LOOMS:
Levers: 1 + 2
       3 + 4

REQUIREMENTS: For an 8 yd. warp to
finish 6 yds. × 28″ wide
> 3 lbs. wool
> 1½ lbs. rayon flake

Scour well

4 harness, 2 pedal

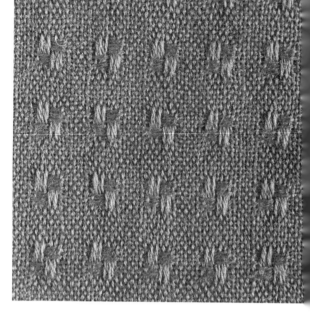

6 harness, 6 pedal

THREADING TIE-UP

2 1

THREADING   TIE-UP

6 5 4 3 2 1

BASKET WEAVE

WARP: Navy 8/2 soft twist cotton @ 3360 yds. per lb.

WEFT: Navy doubled mohair loop, 42% mohair, 58% wool @ 2075 yds. per lb.

WARP ENDS: 720

ENDS PER INCH: 20

REED: 10

WIDTH IN REED: 36″

DENTING: 2 per dent

THREAD: Single in heddle 1, 2, 3, 4

TREADLING: Doubled weft 1, 2

TABLE LOOMS:
Levers: 1 + 2
          3 + 4

REQUIREMENTS: For 1 yd.
Warp 4 oz.
Weft 6 oz.

WARP: Gold 20/2 worsted @ 5600 yds. per lb.

WEFT: Same as warp

WARP ENDS: 864

ENDS PER INCH: 24

REED: 12

WIDTH IN REED: 36″

DENTING: 2 per dent

THREAD: Single in heddle
6, 5 ×4
4, 3 ×2
2, 1 ×2

TREADLING:
1, 2 ×8
3, 4 ×2
5, 6 ×2

REQUIREMENTS: Warp and weft for one yd., 6 oz.

STOLE 4 harness, 2 pedal

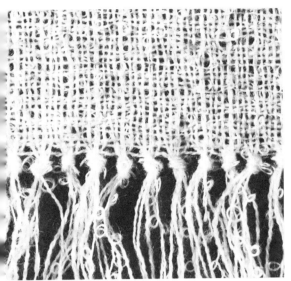

WARP: Natural 20/2 worsted @ 5600 yds. per lb.

Natural mohair loop @ 2400 yds. per lb.

WEFT: Same as warp

WARP ENDS: 390

ENDS PER INCH: 15

REED: 12

THREADING TIE-UP

2 1

WIDTH IN REED: 26″

DENTING: 1 per dent except
2 per dent on harness 1

THREAD: 1, 2, 3, 4

worsted ⎫₁
mohair ⎭

worsted 2

worsted 3

worsted 4

REQUIREMENTS: For 1 stole including loom allowance, 3½ yds. warp

Worsted, 7 oz.

Mohair, 2 oz.

WARPING ORDER: 4 yard warp:

1 worsted

1 mohair ⎫
4 worsted ⎭ ×77

1 mohair

3 worsted

TREADLING: 1, 2

3 worsted 1, 2, 1

1 mohair 2

90″ on the loom

Very light beat

SCARF 4 harness, 2 pedal

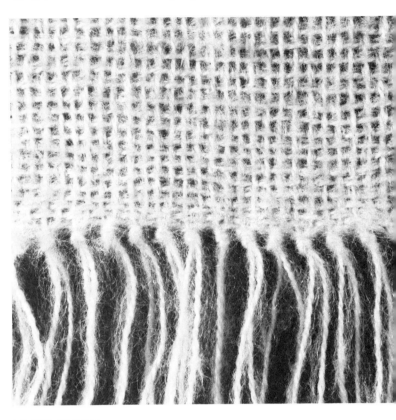

PLAIN WEAVE

WARP: Cream mohair @ approx. 90 yds. per ball

WEFT: Same as warp

WARP ENDS: 48

ENDS PER INCH: 6

REED: 12

THREADING TIE-UP

2 1

WIDTH IN REED: 8″

DENTING:

1 per dent

1 empty dent

THREAD: Single in heddle 1, 2, 3, 4

WARP: For one scarf

1½ yds. + loom allowance

TREADLING: 1, 2

Weave 40″

Very light beat

TABLE LOOMS:

Levers: 1 + 3
2 + 4

REQUIREMENTS: For 1 scarf, 2 yd. warp

1½ balls mohair

(123)

7/2 Douppioni silk @ 5800 yds. lb.

Novelty wool and rayon bouclé

7/1 Wool @ 3900 yds. lb.

12 Cut wool in oil @ 3600 yds. lb.

"Tweed" @ 2700 yds. lb.

Single ply wool in oil @ 2200 yds. lb.

Flecked wool @ 2000 yds. lb.

Mohair Loop @ 2400 yds. lb.

Mohair @ 900 yds. lb.

Eiderdown @ 1900 yds. lb.

"Cable" worsted @ 560 yds. lb.

Swedish Cowhair @ 600 yds. lb.

Norwegian "Ullspissgarn" @ 640 yds. lb.

Persian type 3 strand 2 ply @ 800 yds. lb.

Rug wool @ 225 yds. lb.

Rug wool @ 300 yds. lb.

Rug worsted @ 600 yds. lb.

Rug worsted @ 300 yds. lb.

Rug worsted @ 210 yds. lb.

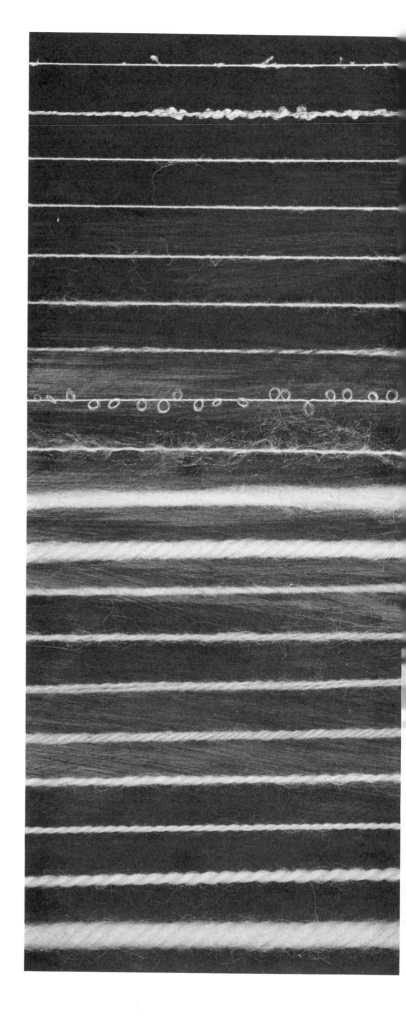

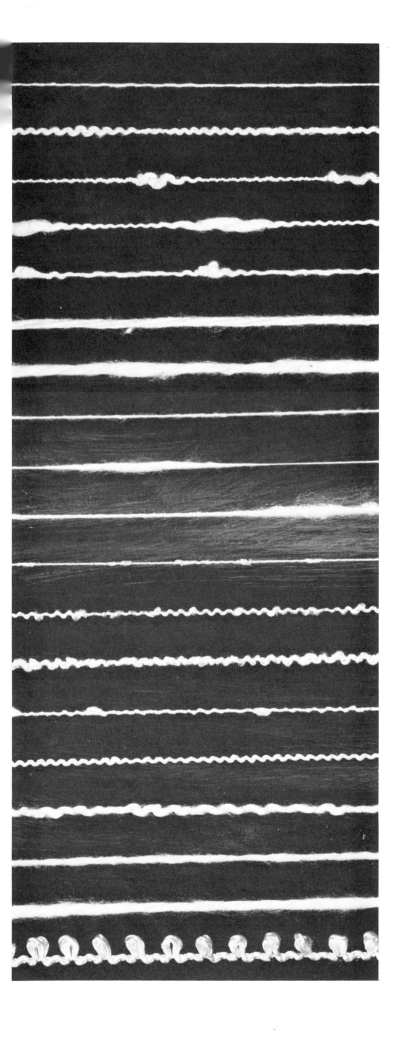

"Cottolin" 54% cotton, 46% linen @ 3250 yds. lb.

Cotton ratine @ 1450 yds. lb.

Cotton flake @ 1700 yds. lb.

Cotton flake @ 1250 yds. lb.

Cotton knot (nub) @ 900 yds. lb.

3 Ply Shiny cotton @ 400 yds. lb.

2 Ply cotton roving @ 600 yds. lb.

Rayon flake @ 4500 yds. lb.

Slub rayon @ 3500 yds. lb.

Slub rayon @ 840 yds. lb.

Rayon bouclé @ 2200 yds. lb.

Rayon bouclé @ 1700 yds. lb.

Rayon-cotton bouclé @ 650 yds. lb.

Rayon knot (nub) @ 1300 yds. lb.

Rayon ratine @ 1700 yds. lb.

Soft spun rayon ratine @ 800 yds. lb.

Wool spun rayon @ 960 yds. lb.

2 Ply soft twist rayon @ 400 yds. lb.

Rayon loop fringe

12 Cut chenille @ 1200 yds. lb.

8 Cut chenille @ 800 yds. lb.

6 Cut chenille @ 600 yds. lb.

3 Cut chenille @ 300 yds. lb.

$^3/_{16}$'' Metallic flatfold @ 375 yds. lb.

Slub linen @ 840 yds. lb.

Viscose @ 1200 yds. lb.

2 Ply spun viscose @ 840 yds. lb.

Single ply jute @ 1200 yds. lb.

2 Ply jute @ 600 yds. lb.

2 Ply jute @ 300 yds. lb.

Jute and viscose @ 1200 yds. lb.

Jute and viscose @ 140 yds. lb.

PERIODICALS

American Craft
American Crafts Council
22 West 55th Street
New York, NY 10019

Fiberarts
50 College Street
Asheville, NC 28801

Interweave
Interweave Press
306 North Washington, Dept. SD
Loveland, CO 80537

Shuttle, Spindle & Dyepot
65 LaSalle Road
West Hartford, CT 06107

The Weaver's Journal
P.O. Box 2049
Boulder, CO 80306

WEAVING TERMS

BEAM—WARP BEAM holds the warp
  BACK BEAM over which the warp passes
  FRONT OR BREAST BEAM over which the web passes
  CLOTH BEAM holds the web.

BEAMING—Winding the warp on the loom.

BEATER—The frame which holds the reed. Used to "beat" the weft into place.

CHAIN—The warp made into a chain for easier handling as it is taken from the warping frame.

CROSS—Alternate crossing of warp threads during warping so that threads are kept in order during beaming and threading.

DENT—A single space in the reed.

DENTING—Spacing warp in the reed.

DRAFT—The threading pattern drawn on graph paper.

DRESSING—Preparing the loom for weaving.

ENDS—Warp threads.

HARNESS—Frame which holds the heddles.

HEDDLE FRAME—Same as "harness."

HEDDLES—Made of steel, wire or string with eyes in the center through which the warp is threaded.

LAMS—Horizontal levers connecting harnesses and pedals.

PEDALS—See treadles.

PICK OR SHOT—One throw of weft thread shuttled through the shed.

REED—A comb-like piece in the beater used to separate the warp threads and to beat the weft into the web.

SCOURING—To wash and rinse woven fabric.

SHED—The opening in the warp, formed by the treadling action, through which the shuttle is thrown.

SPACED WARP—Variations in spacing the warp in the reed.

TABBY—Plain weave. Weft is woven singly over and under each warp thread.

TIE-UP—Refers to the tie connecting harnesses to pedals on floor looms.

TREADLES—Pedals on a floor loom which raise or lower the harness frames.

WARP—Threads which lie lengthwise in the loom.

WARPING—Making the warp.

WEB—Piece of woven cloth.

WEFT—Threads which are woven across the warp.

YARN—Any kind of weaving thread, not necessarily woolen.

YARN SUPPLY SOURCES

American Harvest Yarn
851 Hamilton Avenue
Menlo Park, CA 94025

Belding Lily Company
P.O. Box 88
Shelby, NC 28150

Contessa Yarns
P.O. Box 37, Dept. SD
Lebanon, CT 06249

Cum USA
P.O Box 408F
Sonoma, CA 95476

Frederick J. Fawcett, Inc.
129 South Street
Boston, MA 02111

Fiber Studio
Foster Hill Road
Henniker, NH 03242

Fort Cralio Yarn Co.
2 Green Street, Dept. 3
Rensselaer, NY 12144

Forte Fibers
P.O. Box 818
Palisade, CO 81526

Glass House Fiber Imports
R.D. 2, Box 12
Putney, VT 05346

Greentree Ranch Wools
163 North Carter Lake Road
Loveland, CO 80537

Kiwi Imports, Inc.
P.O. Box 372
Braintree, MA 02184

R. H. Lindsay Company
253 Summer Street
Boston, MA 02210

Lundgren Rya, Inc.
540 West Main Street
Northboro, MA 01532

Manos del Uruguay
35 West 36th Street, Dept. SH
New York, NY 10018

Mission Mill Museum
260 12th Street, SE
Salem, OR 97301

Novitex, Inc.
250 Esten Avenue
Pawtucket, RI 02862

Old Mill Yarn
P.O. Box 8
Eaton Rapids, MI 48827

Oregon Worsted Co.
P.O. Box 02098, Dept. K
Portland, OR 97202

The River Farm
Rt. 1, Box 401
Timberville, VA 22853

School Products, Inc.
1201 Broadway
New York, NY 10001

Scott's Woolen Mill
Dept. F, 90 Elmdale Road
Uxbridge, MA 01569

Solar Spun Yarns
P.O. Box 2143
Jenkintown, PA 19046

Stanley Berroco
2 Elmdale Road, Dept. SSD
Uxbridge, MA 01569

Tinkler & Co., Inc.
Box 17
Norristown, PA 19404

Village Wools
3719 Fourth, NW
Albuquerque, NM 87107

Weaver's Way
306 East Goldsboro Street
Crown Point, IN 46307

John Wilde & Brother, Inc.
3705 Main Street, Dept. S
Philadelphia, PA 19127

LOOM SUPPLY SOURCES

(Firms marked by an asterisk sell both looms and yarns.)

Arachne Looms
Box 174
Whitefish, MT 59937

Cadman Loom Company
P.O. Box 922
Vashon Island, WA 98070

Cascade Looms
7364 Conifer NE
Salem, OR 97303

Dorset Looms
P.O. Box 520
Stillwater, NY 12170

The Fiber Designer Loom
1836 Candelaria NW
Albuquerque, NM 87107

Fireside Looms & Weaving
91600 West Fork Road
Deadwood, OR 97430

Gilmore Looms
1032 North Broadway
Stockton, CA 95205

*Glimakra Loom 'n Yarns, Inc.
P.O. Box 16157 HG2
Rocky River, OH 44116

Green Mountain Creative Crafts
Hinesburg, VT 05461

Handweaving Studio
Box 233
Sedona, AZ 86336

*Harrisville Designs
Main Street
Harrisville, NH 03450

Hearld Looms
100 Lee Street
Lodi, OH 44254

Hickory Ridge Sawmill & Woodcraft
Peterson, MN 55962

J. Made Looms & Weaving Accessories
P.O. Box 452
Oregon City, OR 97045

Kessenich Looms
7463 Harwood Avenue
Wauwatosa, WI 53213

Kyra Loom Co.
110 Duerstein Street
Buffalo, NY 14210

Leclerc Corporation
P.O. Box 491 HW9 N
Plattsburg, NY 12901

Loom Craft
P.O. Box 65
Littleton, CO 80160

Macomber Looms
Beech Ridge Road
York, ME 03909

Northwest Looms
P.O. Box 10369
Bainbridge Island, WA 98110

Norwood Looms
P.O. Box 167-S
Fremont, MI 49412

*OR. Rug Co., Dept. 9080
Lima, OH 45802

Pendleton Shop
Box 233
Sedona, AZ 86336

*Robin & Russ Handweavers
533 North Adams Street
McMinnville, OR 97128

Schacht Spindle Co., Inc.
P.O. Box 2157 K
Boulder, CA 80306

Sievers Looms
Fox Lane
Washington Island, WI 54246

Studio Handcrafts
P.O. Box 686
Tarzana, CA 91356

Tawaquiva
1836 Candelaria NW
Albuquerque, NM 57107

Waconsta
Box 1109
St. George, VT 84770

Willow Tree Looms
Box 108
Lincoln, AR 72744

Zeek's Looms and Woodcraft
4132 Glenwood Drive SE
Salem, OR 97301

INDEX